ZODIAC

SCOTLAND

Edited by Lucy Jeacock

First published in Great Britain in 2002 by
YOUNG WRITERS
Remus House,
Coltsfoot Drive,
Peterborough, PE2 9JX
Telephone (01733) 890066

HB ISBN 0 75433 688 3
SB ISBN 0 75433 689 1

FOREWORD

Young Writers was established in 1991 with the aim of promoting creative writing in children, to make reading and writing poetry fun.

Once again, this year proved to be a tremendous success with over 41,000 entries received nationwide.

The Zodiac competition has shown us the high standard of work and effort that children are capable of today. The competition has given us a vivid insight into the thoughts and experiences of today's younger generation. It is a reflection of the enthusiasm and creativity that teachers have injected into their pupils, and it shines clearly within this anthology.

The task of selecting poems was a difficult one, but nevertheless, an enjoyable experience. We hope you are as pleased with the final selection in *Zodiac Scotland* as we are.

CONTENTS

John Wadsworth	90
Philip Speedie	91
Jayne Fleming	91
Carol Graham	92
Scott Smith	92
Kristoffer Corbett	93
Laura Thomson	93
Rhona Lees	94
Claire Hamilton	94
Lynsay Rennie	94
Gayle Loggie	95
Linsey Sneddon	95
Graeme Smith	95
Laura Dyer	96
Alison King	96
Gareth Kerr	97
Jenna Smith	97
David Hogg	98
Yvonne Jewkes	99
Jill Graham	99
Charlene McInally	100
Arianne Fox	100
Danielle Scott	100
Iain Walker	101
Rachel Simpson	101
Lynsey Douglas	101
Jane McLaren	102
Stephanie Steele	102
Claire Hamilton	102
Andrea McAulay	103
Andrew Marshall	103
Lisa Dyer	103
Fiona Tennant	104
Emma Smith	104
David Morrison	104
Aaron Wark	105
Greig Hawke	105
Graeme Sorbie	105

Jayson M Duncan	106
Natalie Vance	106
Scott Paton	106
Kim Graham	107
Lesley Ballantyne	107
Salaam Ahmad	107
Alison Campbell	108

Lomond School

Josh Coats	108
Jonathan McLatchie	109
Laura McHard	110
Robert Stevenson	110
Robbie Liddell	111
Greig Logan	112
Rebecca Stephenson	113
Craig Kelly	114
Christopher Donnachie	114
Anna Dobson	115
Caroline Wylie	115
Kara Dawson	116
Bethany Apedaile	117
Alicia Barham	118
Kirsty Baynham	119
Rachael Cameron	120
Fiona Milton	121
Abbie Williamson	122
Laura Carver	122
Euan Millar	123
Kirsty Cameron	124
Jenna MacLeod	124

Madras College

Heather Barnes	125
Charis Bredin	126
Jack Shepherd	127
Marcie Sturrock	128

Erica Mackie	240
Laura McKenna	240
Dominic Gillespie	240
Yasumi Takamiyagi	241
Russell King	241
Graeme Paris	241
Mairi Laverty	242
Lori Dempster	242
Craig Allan	243
Ben Higson	243
Daniel Jackson	244
Ashley Cummings	244
Nicola Hamilton	245
Douglas Murphy	245
Iain McNicol	246
Laura Johnston	246
Lorna Robertson	247
Johnny Paterson	247
Lara Thomas	248
Louise Rawding	249
Nicola Kaney	250
Katrina Button	250
David Kerr	250
Megan Tully	251

Wellington School

Suzanne Higton	251
Claire Anderson	252
Joanna Kerr	252
Christopher Watt	253
Abigail Martin	254
Simon Murphy	255
Kristine Kozicki	256
Mary Howie	257

Woodfarm High School

Steven Coyle	258
Barbara Jamieson	259

The Poems

PROGRESS

Strong, silvery, shiny metal
That's what made the scientists settle.
Man-made disasters would never be the same,
Now they'd be worse and scientists would shame.

It's going to be safe they said,
To help humanity is why it's made.

Corruptive eyes filled scientist with glee
But in the end they'd have to flee.

High tech, potent hardware and software
That brought wicked money no one could share.
The question was asked what's it for,
But that was killed in the political war.

Along with Windows, Bill Gates died
It was AAN robotics where the money lied.
From their computer guided homes,
To their artificial sky,
It was them who caused our race to die.

So when the day finally came
The scientist stood in absolute fame.
Awake RR5, awake to the real world
The robot burst to life and uncurled.
For a second you could say it was cool,
That was until the place became a blood pool.
The robot had started to kill instead of protect
A major flow was what the scientist could detect.

No running, no hiding and no free will,
Until the end it was kill, kill, kill.

Haroon Rehman (13)
Alloa Academy

THE DEADLY 11TH

The plane is gaining speed.
It's heading into New York City,
It's coming in awful low,
Watch out everybody!

It's heading for the World Trade Center,
Oh no it's going to hit!
'Pull up,' everybody shouts,
But it's too late.
Crash!

The first tower sways,
And nearly hits the other.
Everybody gasps.
It can't be happening.
But it really has!

Eighteen minutes later
Another plane is coming.
There's panic in the air
Smash!
It's happened again!

The fire engine rushes through,
But there's no way they're going to get up there
but they try.

The fire is burning.
The walls are melting.
The structure can't take this punishment.
The building collapses.
That's more lives lost.

The first tower still stands.
But only for a while.
It crashes to the ground, thousands die,
Who could do this?
Nobody knows.

Michael McGhee (13)
Alloa Academy

11-09-2001

They woke up to an ordinary day,
What was about to pass,
No one could say.

They climbed the stairs to go so high.
But this is where they soon would die.

What did they do?
What did they say?
To stop them seeing another day.

What was the reason for all this sorrow?
What will happen to us all tomorrow?

Are there hopes for the future
Or only fears?
So much sorrow,
So many tears.

Christopher Andrews (13)
Alloa Academy

PLAYING RUGBY

As I stand here bold, but timid
Waiting anxious for the whistle,
Wondering who I'll meet,
Wondering if we'll get beat.

The whistle blows and off we go.
Who will get the hardest blow?
Will we win or will we lose?
Will I go home with a bruise?

I catch the ball and off I run
Like a cheetah in the sun.
I dodge one, two -
I get the try!
The whistle goes,
We say goodbye.

Peter Michie (13)
Alloa Academy

SHOPPING

There's nothing quite like shopping,
To chase your blues away.
It makes you feel all good inside,
Until you've got to pay!

Boys and men hate shopping;
It makes them bored and angry too.
It really comes down to one thing:
They haven't got a clue!

They don't understand the pleasures of shopping,
They really don't see,
The point in going shopping,
Quite different from you and me!

Girls on the other hand,
Are experts, at such a joyful art.
They know all the ins and outs,
Of how people and money part!

Louise Taylor (13)
Alloa Academy

WE'RE AT WAR

Bang! What has happened,
People screaming, crying children,
Dead bloody bodies under the rubble,
A soldier shouts: 'We're at war!'

Grieving people crying aloud,
Split up families, lying around.
People praying on the streets,
Oh God help us please.

Gas alerts, sirens screaming,
Children crying with fear,
What is the world coming to?
So God - help us please!

Claire McGillivray (13)
Alloa Academy

BLOODY BATTLES

Bloody battles, cries of hatred
Help me God! How can this be?
Soldiers shouting: 'Fire, Fire!
Bullets flying - high above.

Children screaming and shouting
Disbelieving finding body parts
Oh help us God! How can this be?
Families destroyed, wondering why?

Gas alert, sirens screeching.
People outside preaching
Fires spreading from town to town
Oh God how can this be?

Louise Barrett (13)
Alloa Academy

ANIMALS, ANIMALS, ANIMALS

Animals, Animals, Animals.
There's nothing quite like animals.
To cheer up your sad lonely day
And make you feel happy and gay.

Animals, Animals, Animals.
There's nothing quite like animals.
Some are friendly some are shy,
You could never pass an animal by.

Jill Ure (13)
Alloa Academy

CITY OF GLASGOW

C   ulmalie was where the heart had lied,
I   t was appealing in all its beauty,
T   he callous land grew scarce and thin,
Y   outh could not live on what was had.

O   ff they went on their quest for life,
F   orever lost as they mount the boat.

G   oing down the narrow riverbank,
L   ong sloping streets back at the horizon,
A   nd defining sounds bouncing off peculiar buildings.
S   hocking heaps of midden,
G   enerations lost in plumes of smoke,
O   n and on people scurry on cobbles,
W   here the hills were, factories tower in
     the city of Glasgow.

Alasdair Gordon (13)
Alloa Academy

WASP

Whizzing
Through the air
Buzz buzz
Attacking people
When annoyed
Swarming
Around people
All day long
Peace at last
The wasp has gone.

David Mathieson (11)
Alness Academy

YOU'RE MY SISTER

You!
Your head is like an empty bottle of rum.
You!
Your eyes are as big as an elephant's bum.
You!
Your ears are as big as The Pentagon.
You!
Your nostrils are as big as a pig's backside.
You!
Your mouth is as wide as the distillery.
You!
Your belly is like the jungle.
You!
You're my sister!

John Auld (12)
Alness Academy

YOU

You
You are as spotted as a Dalmatian
You
You're as mad as a boxer pup.
You
You eat too much.
You
You're as fast as an athlete.
You
You make me happy as can be.
You
You are my pet goldfish called Pongo.

Scott Greenlees (12)
Alness Academy

ARNISDALE

The loch shimmers like crystal,
The seals pop up,
To have a look,
And the porpoises play
Beside the fishing boats.

On Dry Island I stand and see
the whole of the loch.
The crabs scuttle sideways
And shrimps across rock pools.
Otters play beside the pier
Where the big white house stands.
The Highland cows graze.

Look at the little cottages in front of Beinn Sgritheall.
The Royal twelve pointer stands proudly with his herd
in the fields.
The mountains stand all around.
This is Arnisdale.

Anna Jemmett (12)
Alness Academy

MY HERO

I thought you were my hero.
I thought you were really strong.
I thought that you would save me from
Anything, bad or wrong.
I thought you would look out for me
And never leave my sight.
But I guess I thought wrong because
Today you were out of sight.

Christina Stewart (11)
Alness Academy

MY BROTHER

My brother is six years old.
His hair is blond and short.
His name is Robert
And he is very nice.

Robert is smaller than me,
And looks like my Dad.
He loves cheeseburgers
And chips from Burger King.

He loves to play with his friends,
On the tree swing.
I like to read books to Robert,
Like Bob the Builder,
And Postman Pat.

Francesca Donald (13)
Alness Academy

THE MOON

Shining yellow like a banana
Big smiling fort
Like a light bulb
In the dark sky.
Moving slowly
Round the world
Staring at me
I may as well
Let him be.

Lisa McMillan (11)
Alness Academy

FALLING

Falling
Like a bird
To the
Ground
Helpless
Nothing
Can
Stop
M
e
e
e
e
e
e
e
Ouch!

John Fraser (12)
Alness Academy

BOBBY

There was a young man called Bobby,
Who fell in his lobby,
He said it was sore,
When he hit the door,
That stupid man called Bobby.

Bryan Cameron (12)
Alness Academy

YOU!

You!
Your face is like an elephant's.
You!
Your brain is like a pea.
You!
Your eyes are like fireballs.
You!
Your ears are the plane's wings.
You!
Your nostrils are like keyholes.
You!
Your mouth is like a blow horn.
You!
Your arms are like twigs.
You!
Your bum is like a ball of gas.
    But I like *You!*

Kirsty Cooper (11)
Alness Academy

I THOUGHT

I thought you liked me,
I thought you were kind.
I thought you cared,
I thought you were stupid,
I thought you were loving.
I thought wrong!

Debbie MacDonald (12)
Alness Academy

LITTLE MOUSE

There was a little mouse called Squeak,
He lived in the floorboards with a creak.
He had ten daughters and ten sons,
But his wife had long run away.

One night he said to his children,
'Tomorrow we're having some fun.
We'll have a feast with wine and rum
And plenty of currant buns!'

But when it came to dinner,
He was nowhere to be seen.
It seems that he was dinner
To the greedy cat called Killer!

Xanthe Davies (12)
Alness Academy

A RECIPE FOR AUTUMN

Take extravagance of multicoloured leaves
A whirl of the wind
And thin exposed trees.

Add caramel and bronze leaves
Crispy pine cones
And squirrels in search of nuts.

Mix them in a witch's cauldron
In the middle of a gloomy wood,
Then explode them up inside the midnight sky!

Katy Rogerson (12)
Alness Academy

MY HEART OF THE OCEAN

My heart is a wonderful place,
I do not share it very often.
My thoughts are like fish jumping out of the sea.
My heart is a deep, dark and caring place.
It floats on the ocean when I am happy.
It sinks to the bottom when I am sad.
My heart is mine.
I keep it to myself.
My heart is the heart of the ocean.

Julia Magee (12)
Alness Academy

THE BOY

Tom was a boy
That talked too much.
His tongue had twisted,
Out of touch.

The ambulance arrived,
The orthodontist had a look,
'This needs a surgeon,' he said.

As the anaesthetic
Pinched his arm,
'*Ouch*!' he said,
And fell down flat.

His head throbbed,
His tongue no longer,
In his gob.

Thomas Bowman (12)
Alness Academy

YOU

You?
You are as cuddly as a teddy bear.
You?
Your hair is silky and soft.
You?
You make me feel happy.
You?
You run like a tornado.
You?
Your tail is like a baby's feet.
You?
You're my favourite dog.
You?
You're my Tiara.

Mairi Thomson (12)
Alness Academy

YOU!

You.
You have my name.
You.
You always copy me.
You.
You wear the same clothes.
You.
You always wear make-up.
You.
You copy me!

Emma Bryce (11)
Alness Academy

THE RIVER

The stream is a baby
Howling for its food,
Screaming for its Mum,
Smiling when it's good.
The stream is a baby.

The waterfall is a teenager,
Angry, aggressive and wild.
Lashing out at everyone,
Changing from a child.
The waterfall is a teenager.

The sea is an OAP
Slowing fading with its age.
Creeping, crawling once again,
No longer full of rage.
The sea is an OAP.

Jenna McCluskey (12)
Alness Academy

RED

The look on an angry person's face
A dangerous fiery devil
A river of Man U supporters
A thick stream of blood
The fiery stare of a monstrous beast
The sign that danger is near
A sign to stop to a halt.

Sean Baikie (12)
Alness Academy

HAZEL

I have a sister Hazel,
She really is so sweet,
She smiles and says,
'Hello' to everyone she meets.

But sometimes she can be nasty,
And sometimes she can be rude.
She'll pick her nose, scream and shout,
And throw around her food.

But you can't stay angry with Hazel,
When you look into her eyes.
But you'll get mad when you hear
All her bad words and lies!

She sat on a pin one day,
And it gave her a little prick.
Blaming me, she got angry,
And whacked me with a stick!

It hurt so bad,
I couldn't speak.
I could not sit down
For one whole week!

In the end I have to laugh
As I taped her singing in the bath.
When she finds out
She'll be frothing at the mouth.
That's why I'm running
Away from the house.

Nikki Burns (13)
Alness Academy

THE OLD SHOE

An old shoe,
Lying in the gutter.
No owner.
Once well used,
Now torn and ragged.
It once had its day
But now it's over,
Serving not to house feet,
But housing rats instead.

Aidan Maggs (11)
Alness Academy

JAGUAR! (HAIKU)

Thrives in the jungle,
Fishing with his fast, strong paws.
Rosettes on his coat.

Aidan Parker (12)
Alness Academy

CHRISTMAS (HAIKU)

Snow is around us
Covering the hills and fields
Sparkling in the sun.

Ann MacFarlane (12)
Alness Academy

TWINKLE

Twinkle twinkle
Black sheep star
How I wonder who you are
Up and under wool so thick
Fatter than a great big stick
Twinkle twinkle
Black sheep star
How I wonder what you are.

Kimberley Mackay (12)
Alness Academy

LEAVES

L   ightly falling,
E   ffortlessly swaying,
A   llowing to flip and turn,
V   itally needing to rest,
E   nding with a thump,
S   nuggled with the other leaves.

Linda Robinson (12)
Alness Academy

THE BABY SEAL

Where the baby seal lies
On the rocky shore
Sun shining bright
What a delight
To see the seals once more.

Claire Gillies (11)
Alness Academy

FEAR

F   erocious, fighting lions foraging for food,
E   eerie screeching of owls during the night,
A   n angry elephant stomping across the plains towards me,
R   oaring teachers like rumbling of thunder.

Struan Hull (12)
Alness Academy

THE BEACH

The sun glistening on the sea,
The dolphins playing in the water,
The children making sandcastles in the sand,
Bodies baking in the sun like cookies in an oven,
Water splashes against the rocks,
It's a beautiful day at the beach today.

Emma Gray (12)
Alness Academy

CHOCOLATE

Smooth, creamy,
Sweet-tasting.
Bubbling in bars.
Sliding in your mouth.
Like a log down a stream.
Chocolate
Is a mountain of love.

Sinead Riley (12)
Alness Academy

WINTER

W hen it comes to winter, yipee is all I say.
I n the winter all I do is go outside and play.
N earer and nearer,
T ill it comes inside waiting, watching chums.
E ntertaining yes, but not as fun as the wind.
R aining outside. Hurrah it's come,
   winter's made my life such fun.

Lynsey MacKenzie (12)
Alness Academy

FLYING

Air rushing through my hair,
Clouds below, blue above,
Planes and birds passing by,
Nowhere to go, nothing to do,
I was there,
High in the air,
Air was rushing through my hair.

Louise Urquhart (11)
Alness Academy

THE TREE

Your leaves are as red as a fire,
Brown, yellow, orange.
Are falling from your branches,
The wind is carrying them through the air,
Swirling, gliding, floating to the ground.

Kevin Smith (12)
Alness Academy

I'VE GOT WRITER'S CRAMP!

I've got writer's cramp!
What to write I can't decide.
It's tearing me up inside.
Pen to paper,
Nothing happens,
Help!
What am I going to do?
Maybe I'll write an acrostic,
Or maybe even a limerick.
Oh! I don't know what to do,
Please help me!

I've got writer's cramp
I know I can write something,
But what?
There're colour poems,
And shape poems.
Maybe I'll write a haiku.
Please, please help me!

I've got writer's cramp,
I've got it bad.
Maybe I won't write a poem,
That's what I'll do.
No one will notice,
Will they?

Judith Long (12)
Alness Academy

YOU!

Your face is a donkey's ass.
Ugly!
You!
Your eyes are golf balls
Heading for a hole in one.
You!
Your ears are dumbo's ears.
Big enough to fly.
You!
Your head is a bowling ball.
Big round and shiny.
You!
Your belly is a bowl full of jelly.
Moving all the time.
You!
Your bum is a huge rolling boulder.
Flattening everything in its way.
You!

Elicia Richards (12)
Alness Academy

THERE WAS A YOUNG MAN FROM RYE

There was a young man from Rye,
Who sat on an apple pie,
He started to mumble,
And fell with a tumble,
The apple pie was now crumble.

Robert Hope Fairbairn (12)
Alness Academy

TRUTH OR DARE

There once was a boy and a girl
They wanted to play truth or dare.
So it's the girl's turn, and she picked truth,
And they both told a secret (That you're not to hear of).

Next it was the boy's turn, and he picked dare.
They both could not think
                              think
                                          think
So they decided to leave it there.

Julie Brown (12)
Alness Academy

WORLD WAR III

World War III is here today
'Oh no' there's lots to say.
Rowdy crowds all around the street
Lots of blood around my feet.
Dying people all around
Women and children lying on the ground.
Anger and fear on George Bush's face
Red puddles of blood - oh what a disgrace!
Trembles and shudders sound really near
Hope of finding our loved ones out here.
Rush out of this place, there's nowhere to go
Everyone wait this'll only take a mo!
Everyone awaits and hopes it's not bad
10,000 were killed and it's just so sad!

Sarah-Jane Lafferty (13)
Alva Academy

PERDITION

Trapped inside this lifeless cell,
Locked inside my own mental hell,
there is no way of escaping
this perdition of my own making.
Guarding this prison is my paranoia.
I am my own life destroyer,
But I like to blame my problems on others,
Hide away from the guilt, and
Duck head under the covers.
I believe in Christianity,
Religion enforces my insanity.
I'm climbing the walls, I'm going mad,
I'm remembering everything that I had.
Read the papers, watch TV,
They just fuel my insecurities.
I find myself to be my only friend.
Will things ever improve for me?
I guess I'll have to wait and see.

Colin Davidson (13)
Alva Academy

MIDDLE OF THE NIGHT

A play the drums
'bout an 'oor a day
annoyin' the neighbours
across the way.
They shout an' they scream
and they want a fight,
when a play ma drums
in the middle of the night.

Jordan Hodgson (15)
Alva Academy

MORNING ROUTINE

The sun peeps through the curtains
And the birds cheep in the morning,
And the cars broom broom away to work.
The alarm clock goes off, bleep, bleep.
Time to get up.

I get up and walk down the stairs,
Trying not to fall over.
Mum says 'Hi' as I begin to eat my breakfast.
Snap and crackle and pop.
I get my little sister up by putting my music on full blast.
Then when I'm ready,
I get out the house,
And walk down to the bus stop.

Emma Leitch (12)
Alva Academy

SEPTEMBER 11TH 2001

People   Sudden
Walking   Crashes
People   Sudden
Talking   Flashes
Going   Building
Into   Tumbles
Work   Down

The fear and terror in their eyes
As they fall from the skies.

Kerrie Langdon (13)
Alva Academy

THE SNIPER WW2

As the sniper prepares for his 666th kill.
He slowly prepares himself
rubbing green, brown and black paint on his face.
He slowly rubs his rifle in black soot,
as one glint of light could cause him a bullet in the head.
The sniper sets off at 4am
Quickly scuttling in and out of the debris.
Crawling in a pool of dead bodies he takes his position,
Awaiting his prey.
As he awaits
as still as the dead of night,
he puts snow in his mouth
so the enemy can't see his breath.
The leader of the German army approaches,
walking like a hero
as proud as the first man on the moon.
He takes aim,
Bang
The leader of the German army ceases to exist.

Craig Longwell (14)
Alva Academy

BIG BREAK

I play snooker
from June to May
hoping to be a professional one day.
My aim is to be number one,
but at the moment I'm playing more for fun.
Sure I'll get there some day!

Barry Wraith (15)
Alva Academy

THE DAY THAT CHANGED MY LIFE

It was a normal Tuesday morning,
Everything was fine.
I worked on the seventeenth floor of the World Trade Center,
Everything was fine.
I took the lift up to my office,
Everything was fine
I sat down and turned on my PC,
Everything was fine.
Phones ringing, people chatting,
Everything was fine.
I got a cup of coffee,
Everything was fine.
All of a sudden, *bang!*
Not everything was fine.
I panicked!
Not everything was fine.
Fifteen minutes later *bang* again,
Not everything was fine.
I got out of the building safely,
Not everything was fine.
The Trade Centers were on fire,
Everything was terrible!
Then all of a sudden the buildings fell down,
Everything was terrible!
This was the day that changed my life,
The famous World Trade Centers had fallen down.
More than buildings had collapsed,
It felt like everything was dead.

Steven Crawford (13)
Alva Academy

FROM THE HEART

Everything was perfect
we started out as friends,
I was happy to be around you,
Then my feelings grew.
I tried to blank them
but they were too strong.
Soon I learned you felt the same
suddenly these feelings weren't so bad.
Things began to look up,
we became so close,
you filled me with joy.
I entered the illusion everything would be fine,
but fate played its card.
It struck me like a ton of bricks,
you backed away from me,
you broke my heart.
I couldn't understand it, didn't want to.
I just wanted you back
But, it was not to be.
Today my heart is broken still
time is supposed to heal all wounds
but I don't believe it.
I loved you . . . I still do.
This is from the heart.

Lyn Dimmock (16)
Alva Academy

WORLD TRADE BUILDINGS

World War III in the making
Overhead planes crash
Right into the sides of the Twin Towers
Landing on the people below
Down it comes.

The world is shocked
Running people try to hide.
All the emergency services go up
Down come the injured
Everyone is shocked, crying, many killed.

But where are the terrorists?
Underground they hide
In the rubble the injured lie
Lost in the dust.
Do we strike back?
Is World War III starting?
No one knows who did this
Get the lot before the war starts
Should we strike back?

Alastair Kerr (15)
Alva Academy

GRANDAD

G   reat at war, strong and willing to fight,
R   uling his men to success.
A   cting responsible yet calm.
N   ever thinking he would lose.
D   ead people lying in front of him.
A   s men run towards him with guns.
D   oes not fear anything, for he is the leader.

Callum Scobbie (15)
Alva Academy

SCHOOL TEACHERS

S chool hard
C old classrooms
H ot classrooms
O ut at lunch down the park
O utside playing instead of doing your homework
L ove homework (*not*)

T eachers can be nice especially English
E ating in class is banned by teachers
A pproaching a teacher using bad language
C arrying on gets you a row
H aving fun with homework (*not*)
E at at break but don't drop the rubbish
R otating around geography, modern studies
and history.
S chool is boring at the beginning and fun at the end.

Sarah Leitch (12)
Alva Academy

LOVE

Love is happiness,
Love feels like silk,
Love tastes like passion fruit,
Love looks like a delicate flower
Opening fresh in spring.
Love smells like sweet strawberries,
Love sounds like the first laugh,
From a baby.
Love is happiness.

Nicole Paton (15)
Alva Academy

11TH SEPTEMBER
A DAY TO REMEMBER

Nobody knows who
Nobody knows why
Now thousands are dead
Not one said goodbye.

Five planes went missing
Four planes have crashed
Three buildings fell down
One democracy was mashed.

With buildings up in flames
The skyline soon turned black
With airports closing down
Holidaymakers couldn't get back.

Nobody knows who
Nobody knows why
Now thousands are dead
Not one said goodbye.

Morag Crichton
Alva Academy

IT WIZ NAE ME

Smash
Run, run!
The police are here!
The gangs of the inner city.
Peg it up the street.

The 5-0 screech round the corner
Get out and chase us
Bang, the police door slams
'It wiz nae me.'

Ian Crawford (15)
Alva Academy

THE FIGHT

Her eyes make me shiver,
Her voice makes me quiver,
And she's coming towards me,
Quicker and quicker.
My legs are now jelly,
So I'm standing still,
But the bully is here,
Ready to kill.
The first punch is thrown,
And I'm in the way,
The second's a kick,
And I'm going to pay.
I scream the word help,
But the crowd just step back,
I'm now on the ground,
And I'm given a whack.
Then she gets up,
And leaves me alone.
The crowd have all followed,
And I'm on my own.
Again.

Gemma Knox (12)
Alva Academy

THE PUNNY

I got sent hame from school wan dae fur misbehavin'
I got a punny
But I found it rather funny.
Ma maw went spare
But I didnae care.
I put the punny in ma trews
But the next thing I knew
Ma trews were in the machine.
Ma punny was all soggy
But ma maw didnae gie a foggy.
I could see it noo . . .
Four belts across ma paw
I thought, thanx a lot maw.

Lyndsey Hamilton (14)
Alva Academy

GARGOYLES

Day is gone, night will come.
Okay for a few, scary for some.
As the stone gargoyles come to life,
Every night continues the strife.
As these creatures begin to live,
Awake from the stone and become massive.
Climb and glide to their hearts delight,
And they're gone and out of sight.
They are defenders of the night.

Stewart Drummond (14)
Alva Academy

PARADISE?

There is a planet covered with land and water.
Full of beautiful flying creatures.
Creatures on the land and in the ocean.
Full of flowers and trees.
You would have thought this world was perfect.
Is it?
There are creatures on the land who would kill for war,
                                    money and land.
These creatures are the worst,
The worst of all creatures.
There is hatred: although there is love.
There is take: although there is give.
There is life: although there is death.
Some day this planet will be destroyed.
Don't know when,
Don't know how,
But it will come.
Could it be from outer space?
The sun, asteroids or black holes?
Could it be from their own devices?
Pollution, war, or greed?
If only this world were perfect,
Just as it was meant to be.

Danielle Williams (14)
Alva Academy

ROAST MY DREAMS

Roast my dreams on the fire
Explode in my domain
Kill my brothers and sisters
I no longer feel the pain.

There are people who keep on waiting
People with hope in their hearts
You have emblazoned great terror
From which few people part.

People over the world
Are joining hands, they unite
In prayer, in support, in comfort.
After you set their world alight.

The President is poised and waiting
Anxious for a reply
Will we take part in combat?
Or rest as innocent people die.

Who knew three planes could cause such destruction
Mere carriers in the sky
In the hands of the wrong people
Twenty thousand people die.

Katie Borthwick (14)
Auchinleck Academy

EVACUATION

Evacuation
Welcome home. House.
Grey, cold-coloured school
dinnerhall, chatting, crockery, filling,
quiet, open, lush. Garden.
Room, palace, my own kingdom.
Pack my life into a bag and go.

Soft inviting bed.
View amazing, breathtaking yet simple,
football, thud, grass below my feet.
heart pounding, sight, swoosh, golf!
evacuation.
Rise and shine morning music.
Heaven forbid those days should come again.

Blair Anderson (15)
Auchinleck Academy

MEMOIRS

Packing my life into a bag
Evacuation.
Family. Loyalty. Belonging. Love.
The tender arguments of affection.
Photographic treasure. Gone.
The fitting feeling of family.
Trustworthy, forever friends.
Circle memories of a life passed.
The comfort of home.
Rings gone. Precious memories.
Secure home. Family house.
Familiar surroundings now gone.
Evacuation.

Forbidden days have come again.

Deborah McTaggart (14)
Auchinleck Academy

EVACUATION

The morning wake of Sunday bells.
Black. Depression. Silent. Lack.
Evacuation.
The familiar scents of the ones you love,
Sweet fresh smell of tidyness.
Music. Quiet. Relaxing. Music.
Beautiful noise of screaming children laying.
Pack my life into a bag and go.
Secrets that everyone knows.
Oil burning. Mum. Oil burning. Work.
Heaven forbid these days should come again.
Cold fire. Burning sparklers spit.
Evacuation.

Kerry Ho (14)
Auchinleck Academy

EVACUATION

The laughter of fun in the street.
Mum. Dad. Mum. Dad.
Evacuation.
Heaven forbid those days should come again.
The music singing my songs.
Room. Space. No more.
The dog barking when I come home. Jake.
Comfortable. My bed.
Pedals. Wheels. My bike.
The garden grass.
Pack my life into a bag and go.
It's my life.

Adam Frew (15)
Auchinleck Academy

TEMPEST FOR A TRAITOR

Bent beyond the reaches of possibility
They snapped.
Thinnest tracing cracks race
They explode outward
Like a bottle on stone.
Tiniest pebble to a landslide
In an instance.

Anger
Turmoil
Thunderclouds built up
Miles out at sea
Then unleashed
With the force of vengeful gods
Explosions of blue-white-purple.

Bitter gusts whip up
Briny waves
And fling them at the shore
Reaching ever for the cliffs
Hungry for the land . . .

But for you
Only a tear
No more.

No more.

Kelly Forbes (16)
Berwickshire High School

MY COUSINS

My cousins are annoying
They drive me up the wall.
Because they are bossy.
My cousin from Jersey is really really sweet.
His name is Callum.
He is only two years old.

Katie Wilson (12)
Carrongrange School

MINCE AND TATTIES

I'm never late
When there's mince and tatties on my plate.
When I finish school
I feel so cool.
I run all the way home
To eat it!

Ian Crawford (11)
Carrongrange School

I AM . . .

I open my heart and I open my eyes,
But all that I see through my unseeing eyes,
Are dark clouds so black and dismal grey skies,
I'm blind.

I ready my ears to listen to sound,
But all that I hear are the thunderous clouds.
I cannot hear but it's oh so loud,
I'm deaf.

I hobble along and I try to stand,
But always shall, I need someone's helping hand.
Never will I rise tall, great and grand,
I'm lame.

I look up and I swat at the thing,
But no matter how hard I hit,
It never seems to be there - never there is it.
I'm insane . . .

Thomas Gow (12)
Dollar Academy

11TH SEPTEMBER 2001

Osama bin Laden:
Could he be the man
Who caused death and destruction
And mourning throughout the land?

First the towers shake,
And then the towers fall,
Once there were two skyscrapers,
Now there's nothing at all.

Could this be World War Three?
A very frightening thought!
What will happen next
If revenge is sought?

Thousands perhaps dead,
Could be even more,
If America decides,
To fight a holy war.

Fiona Butterfield (12)
Dollar Academy

MY KITTEN

I have a beautiful kitten
He is as soft as a
black satin mitten.

His name is Angel
but that's not how he acts
with his friends
who are grown up cats.

He is as black as
the darkest night with
bright green eyes
the same shade as
sun bleached grass.

If he is out
he bounces around on
his delicate yet
dangerous paws.

With his sharp little ears
he can hear when you're near.

He purrs when he's happy,
warm and sleepy
and miaows when he's stressed
or feeling a little weary.

He can also get cheeky
or even get smart,
but I'd hate it for us
ever to part.
He is one year old
and he is always being told
to try and like the vet
and that he's my special pet.

I'll love him in the morning
I'll love him at night,
he sleeps under my covers
and I tell him sleep tight.

Angel is so cute that he
is as cute as can be
and I could probably say
he means the world to me.

Zoe Moir (12)
Gleniffer High School

A STORMY NIGHT

Boom, bash, boom, crash
There I saw another flash
Counting up 6, 7, 8, 9, 10
There I hear the roar again.

Boom, bash, boom, crash
Everywhere I see a flash
I hear the rain
Go down the drain.

Boom, bash, boom, crash
It's splishing and it's sploshing
My mum can't hang out the washing.

Boom, bash, boom, crash!

Robbie Carter (13)
Gleniffer High School

A MAN'S BEST FRIEND

A suckling fur ball
A baby so small.

A little nipper
A chewer of slippers.

An ear licker
A flea picker.

A bone biter,
A playful fighter.

A buddie to the end
A man's best friend.

A catalogue to make
                    me a dog.

Sarah McNamara (11)
Gleniffer High School

A BIRD

Up and down,
down and up,
round and round,
swoosh.
Hover, hover,
chirp and squawk,
peck then nip,
flap.

Katy Speirs (12)
Gleniffer High School

LIFE

Life, what is life?
Riding on a bike?
Doing homework?
Trying to think?
Building a kitchen sink?
Writing or fighting?
Taking drugs?
Dropping mugs?
Death, what is death?
Going to Heaven or cloud no 7?
Going to Hell and finally can't tell how you died?
You maybe got fried?
Maybe you ate something so big you will suffocate?
Live life to the max and pay your tax!

So don't waste it,
Embrace it!

Christopher Rankin (12)
Gleniffer High School

LASSIES

L   adies night
A   nd I'm out in the town
S   oaring through clubs
S   inging karaoke
I   n the pubs
E   very time I dance with them
S   eriously hot stuff.

Craig Bickertaff (13)
Gleniffer High School

MY DAD

My dad is a pain
Lazy is his nickname.

He goes out nearly every Saturday night,
and when he comes in, he looks a sight.

He's never grumpy, he never moans,
he always smiles and never groans.

I love him very much but I may not show it well,
he was always there when I grazed my knees and fell.

Don't think I hate him, don't think I'm bad,
I love him very much and he never makes me sad.

Remember I love him, remember I care,
Remember I'll always be there.

Lyndsay Campbell (13)
Gleniffer High School

CHRISTMAS

C   is for the Christmas tree sitting in the corner.
H   is for the happiness that we all share.
R   is for the reindeer flying all around.
I   is for the icicles hanging from the roof.
S   is for the snow lying on the ground.
T   is for the toys lying all around.
M   is for the mistletoe hanging on the walls.
A   is for the angels singing Christmas songs.
S   is for the stockings hanging on the walls.

Gael MacKenzie (13)
Gleniffer High School

TERRIFYING PLANE INCIDENT

You set off on your plane ride away to paradise,
Pilot says, 'There's a change of plan,'
Then you all freeze like a block of ice.
Four men come out of the passengers' seats,
They threaten everybody with their knives,
Then you hear some beats,
They are going to take all our lives.
Everyone is screaming,
We're all going to die.
Everybody is phoning
All their families.
You looked out of the window,
You saw a building 130 storeys high.
You got closer and closer,
You all shut your eyes,
And?

Niall Blair (12)
Gleniffer High School

WORLD WAR I

We are sitting in the trenches waiting for the order
The order is sound and is echoing through the trench
Up and over we go.
The guns are shot, there are bullets flying past me
There is carnage all around me
Men screaming in pain
People retreating back to the trenches.

Christopher Woolfries (13)
Gleniffer High School

SEPTEMBER 11TH 2001

Flames rose high into the sky,
Many people knew they would die,
Burns and bruises, emotional trauma,
People leapt from multi-storey buildings in New York.

The 11th of September,
Is a day the world will remember.
Many people lost their lives,
Others their children and their wives.

People left lots of flowers,
To mourn what happened at the towers.
Now the world must wait,
While Bush and Blair decide world fate.

Danielle McMaster (12)
Gleniffer High School

LORRAINE

L   is for my big sister, Lorraine.
O   K she can be moody who cares?
R   enfrewshire Council, she works there.
R   ight under my nose she is every day.
A   lways I will be nice to her,
I   f she's nice to me.
N   ot one thing she does wrong.
E   vil little brother, but nice big sister -
          Lorraine

Lauren Campbell (13)
Gleniffer High School

FOOTBALL

Running, running, got the ball
Oh no, not now, going to fall.
Crying, crying, it's not fair,
So I stand up and shout and swear.
We've no chance now we're 4-0 down,
but I say wait we'll beat them down
until we can win the game.
It's only half-time I said to them
We hacked and hacked and hacked until
We're four goals up, oh this is brill,
but now 5-4-3-2-1-nil.
The game is over, that was fast,
Now I'll run home and tell my dad.
We won I'll say by just one goal
but we got tons and tons of fouls.
So we won the game and had a laugh,
but I'm all mucky, so I'll have a bath,
and when I'm in bed all warm and snuggly,
I'll have good dreams, for tomorrow I am playing Rugby.

Robert Parker (12)
Gleniffer High School

THE MATHS LESSON

S creaming children running riot,
C alm teachers not having rows.
H aving punnies given out puts them in a bad mood.
O n the desks are all our work.
O ut the classroom goes the bad boy,
L eaning and sulking on the table, we are all bored.

Mark McGuinness (13)
Gleniffer High School

THE QUIET

The quiet drags on,
alone, in the darkness
slowly going mad,
still staring, the quiet goes on.

Still quiet, the silence is interrupted,
by a tap dripping slowly,
like blood dripping softly,
slowly but still in madness, confusion,
the quiet drags on.

Now, the quiet interrupted,
not just by the drip,
but by the howling of wolves.
Softly faintly
finally going mad,
the quiet goes on alone,
in a dark, cold, mountain cabin,
the quiet drives you insane.

Grant Paton (11)
Gleniffer High School

IT'S TERRIBLE

It's terrible, people screaming,
Everyone is in shock,
Did that actually happen?
Help us, help us, save America.

I turn around, it's terrible.
They are on fire, two towers collapsing.
Help us, help us, save America.

Suzanne Wylie (13)
Gleniffer High School

ICE HOCKEY

The puck is dropped
The clock's not stopped,
Now the play begins.
He skates down the ice,
The goalie comes out,
But the fans all shout,
And when the team all cheer
Then they all shout goal!

The defenders are back
But the forwards are flat
Now the forwards jump up
But now see them score a
Goal!

David Stafford (11)
Gleniffer High School

ST MIRREN

F   antastic
O   opponents
O   ppose
T   ackling
B   arging
A   nd
L   ots of
L   egs

T   ouchlines
E   xciting to watch
A   wesome players
M   ean
S   coring.

Stuart Pollock (12)
Gleniffer High School

CATS AND DOGS

The ultimate battle
Of cats and dogs.
The ultimate struggle
Of mutts and mogs.

The pain, the horror,
Oh yes, the horror.
I hate to think
What they do with their collars.

Are they to strangle?
Does it help in their plan?
Or are they just bands
For the best friend of man?

If cats rule us all
The world will end.
We're depending on dogs
Man's best friend.

Stephen Smith (11)
Gleniffer High School

SCARED

S   olitary
C   aged in
A   ll alone
R   eally frightened
E   asily could drown
D   eath

I'm so glad that that was only a dream.

Paul McGivern (12)
Gleniffer High School

BEDTIME

When I go to bed at night I switch off my light
and hope I sleep all through the night.

Creaking of the floorboards squeaking of the mouse,
all these noises in my house.

My imagination is running riot,
I wish my house was nice and quiet.

You think there's something under your bed
Scary thoughts going through your head.

You try your best to get to sleep
but always have to have a peek.
Then on the curtains you see his face
It disappears without a trace.
Back again his dark eyes stare,
Then you see his straggly hair.

Then in the morning it's all nice and bright,
Not scary like it is at night.
You can hear birds singing in the blue skies.
The curtains have patterns.
They're not hair and eyes,
It's just your imagination telling you lies.

Jennifer Montgomery (11)
Gleniffer High School

MY FAMILY

There are three other people who live with me,
Those three I call my family.
There's Mum, Dad and my big brother and
I know I'll love them for ever and ever.

Joanne Garbutt (11)
Gleniffer High School

NIGHT AWAKE

Silence, then a creak,
Like the roar of a wounded animal.
Dripping, the dripping of the blood of your soul,
Screaming, screaming for this reason untold.
Scraping, scraping of the knife on the edge of a table.
Silence, the deafening silence.
Time drags like the dragging of your feet on the floor.
You hear footsteps, you look out the window.
Nothing is there.
Then, then you think it's over
The clocks tick, raising the hairs on the back of your neck.
Then the horror is over
Until the night comes.

John Murphy (12)
Gleniffer High School

DISASTER

(Written in memory of the people who died in the American disaster).

D   evastation all around,
I   njured people, lying on the ground.
S   obbing survivors, run for their life,
A   s others stand in disbelief.
S   moke fills the air and covers people,
T   ears flow from eyes of injured people.
E   mbers fall and people bow their heads, to
R   espect all of the innocent dead.

Johnathan Mullan (12)
Gleniffer High School

THE BABOON IN MY ROOM

Last night when I got home,
I went to use the phone,
The line was dead,
I heard my mum shout,
'Get to your bed!'
I went upstairs,
And into my room,
Where there sat,
A rather large baboon!
I looked at him,
And he looked at me.
He got such a fright,
He bit my knee!
Then I screamed . . .
And so did he.

I ran into my parents' room.
When I came back,
Where was that baboon?
I ran into the dining room,
Where there stood,
That baboon!
Then I grabbed a small teaspoon
And hit him on the head,
He was out cold . . . so . . .
I took him outside and thought . . .
Is he dead?
When I woke up next morning,
He was not there,
But on the step,
In the place of the baboon,
There was a 'Big', 'Fluffy' *bear!*

Sheree McPherson (11)
Gleniffer High School

REALITY OF LIFE

R eal life is hard sometimes
E ven adults have hard times.
A dults are humans too.
L ife is a precious thing.
I n my lifetime.
T here have been terrorist attacks, wars and more.
Y es, all this has happened in *my lifetime!*

Lynsay Murphy (13)
Gleniffer High School

AUTUMN

A ll the leaves fall,
U nder the trees, children kick leaves.
T rees are brown, red and green,
U nder the roof of the house children are asleep.
M orning light appears,
N ow a new day of autumn reappears.

Kirsty Scott (13)
Gleniffer High School

DISASTER

D eath all around us.
I n working hours.
S mell of death.
A ll those people dead.
S hocked faces.
T ears in our eyes.
E veryone screaming.
R eal life.

Jacqueline Paterson (12)
Gleniffer High School

THE MOON

A big full moon is very bright,
It sends the wolves out howling at night.
Some nights, it's halved,
Or doesn't seem to be there.
But honestly it is,
It's just hiding somewhere.

Lauren McIntyre (12)
Gleniffer High School

SEASONS

Ho how hot the sun of summer,
That wakens everything.
But how cold the winter
That makes everyone sleep in.
I wish every day would be like the summer,
Then I could wake up with a spring.

Callum Young (12)
Gleniffer High School

ROLLY

Rolly Polly barks and plays,
That's how he spends his days.
Running up, up and down the street
biting people's feet.
My feet he does not touch
because I'll kick his butt!

Isabella Donnell (12)
Gleniffer High School

SPACE

The universe is a mysterious place;
Maybe the home of another race.
Full of beautiful planets and twinkling stars,
No wonder we are trying to visit Mars!

Neptune, Uranus, to name but a few,
Some planets yellow, some planets blue.
Multicoloured planets and hurtling comets,
The planet of Jupiter has a hurricane upon it!

The Milky Way, galaxy and beautiful constellations,
They all mean a lot to me.
Maybe one day we will find other planets,
And hopefully we will find more people like ET!

Jennifer Laird (12)
Gleniffer High School

CATS

So many shapes and sizes,
So many colours and kinds.
Cats have different characters,
Whether they have the same mind.

Cats keep warm with their thick fur,
When warm they're happy and decide to purr.
They have the sharpest claws,
For shoes, pink padded paws.

My favourite cats are cute and fluffy,
Sometimes cuter than a puppy.

Nicola Hyndman (12)
Gleniffer High School

SCHOOL DINNERS

It's eleven o'clock and I feel hungry.
It feels like a long week, but it's only just Monday.
It's been so long since I ate my toast
I'm beginning to think I can see a ghost.
I wonder what's for dinner,
I contemplate.
It's got so bad I can't concentrate.
Macaroni cheese, fish and chips,
Pizza, salad or cheesy dip.
Not long now, I can hardly wait.
I'll be down those stairs and through that gate.
Waiting over - lunch begins
I could eat a million things.

Lauren McKay (12)
Gleniffer High School

NETBALL

N   is for net aim the ball high
E   is for energy that's what netballers need.
T   is for team that's what I mean.
B   is for ball that I hit against the wall.
A   is for attendance, to be there every night.
L   is for luck that you need for a match.
L   is for losers if we lose but that never happens
    'cause we're number 1.

Lynsey Clark (13)
Gleniffer High School

THE RACE

Poetry isn't really my thing
I could sit all day
Not knowing what to say
I have to write about something I like.

So what do I like?

I like to run
To feel the wind on my face
Blowing my hair all over the place
To feel the buzz of the race
Trying to keep up the pace.

Almost there,
Keep going, keep going.
The finishing line is in my sight.
Do I have enough strength to keep up the fight?
Keep going, keep going.

I know I can do it
Finish this race.
Maybe not win
But get second place.
Well, I can dream, can't I?

Jennifer Niven (12)
Gleniffer High School

NEW YORK

The Twin Towers fell from the sky,
Everyone watched as objects flew by.
Nowhere to run, nowhere to hide
Nowhere to go except inside.

New York dim and grey
Thousands of people have died today.
What has happened we cannot forget,
What can we do about this terrible threat?

Nicholas Jones (12)
Gleniffer High School

DREAMLAND

I wake up in the morning
I have to have a wash.
Unfortunately I hear a voice giving me no choice.

I really can't believe it,
I had a bath last night.
What can possibly have happened,
In the middle of the night.

I look in the mirror,
I stand back aghast.
I can't quite believe it,
But I do need a bath.

I sat back and wondered of,
The many dreams I had.

Could it be possible I really went to Mars,
Or won the World Cup?

It really can't be possible,
I stand back in alarm.
Could it be possible it really happened?

It is just unexplainable,
Like tons of other things.

Christopher McCann (11)
Gleniffer High School

SPACE

Space is the darkness, the black holes and stars
Space is the Earth, Jupiter and Mars.
Space is planets and galaxies
Space is meteorites and the Milky Way.

Non-gravity lifting you off your feet
The brightness of the sun as it sits proudly on its throne.
The crisp, quiet air,
          What is it like out in space?

Laura McMillan (12)
Gleniffer High School

IF I WERE

If I were a lion I'd snarl and growl,
If I were a wolf I'd howl and howl,
If I were a cheetah, I'd run very fast,
If I were a tortoise I'd be lost.
If I were a dog I'd bark and bark,
If I were an owl I'd come out at dark.
If I were a mouse I'd scurry and squeak,
And if I were a duck I'd have a beak.
But I am a human as glad as can be,
And I am happy just being *Me!*

Kerrin Rankin (11)
Gleniffer High School

LOOKING AT THE MOON

Floating high in the sky
Like a big bright light shining over the land.
The face of a man with large shining eyes.
Silver in colour as round as a ball, but larger in size.
Out in space with no one near.
What would it be like on the dusty surface of the moon.
The sails in the sky from east to west,
And he never takes a rest.

Danielle Leitch (11)
Gleniffer High School

THE MOON

I can see you, can you see me?
Can you see this man in me?
I hate the sun, it hates me,
But together we make a family.

I wonder why I wonder where
Am I, am I in the air?
Can you see me?

I can see you
But only at night.
So shhh turn off that light.
Then you'll see me even more bright!

Lynsay Milne (12)
Gleniffer High School

A Bonfire Party

Swish goes the Catherine wheel
Bang go the rockets.
There's all the money from the people's pockets.

The sky is dark
Then flash a burst of light
Another big firework taking flight.

After the long and anxious wait
The bonfire is set alight.
A pressuring great hissing as the
fire roars into sight.

Jennifer Corbitt (12)
Gleniffer High School

Pizza

My least favourite food is pizza.
Not the leaning tower of Pisa.
It looks very slimy
I think it's all grimy,
And according to me it all stinks.
Cheese, tomato, pepperoni,
Ham, pineapple and salami.
These are the toppings of a pizza.

Ross McGillivray (11)
Gleniffer High School

CHRISTMAS EVE!

The snowflakes drifted down,
into the small town.
Everything was white,
as bright as a light.

Christmas trees were up with lights shining
with fairies at the top watching people dining.
Children singing carols all day,
while people went out to play.
Christmas Day was on its way.

Alexis Wilson (12)
Gleniffer High School

CATS

I have two cats
I think they are swell.
Their names are Miller and Dre.
They run about like mad at night
And sleep all through the day.
They have a dish full of food.
My mum says they weigh a ton,
But I don't care.
I love them both
They are a lot of fun.

Heather Wilson (11)
Gleniffer High School

FOOTBALL

The buzz when the ball
Hits the back of the net.
The feeling the player
Will never forget.
He takes the ball
He shoots, he scores!
What a noise
As the whole crowd roars.
It really was a brilliant shot.
The manager roars 'This striker's hot!'
The ball is played through
He's got time and space.
Oh no! He's missed.
What a red face!
Oh! That tackle was
Really quite hard.
This may result
In a yellow card.
The match is over now,
They've won the cup.
As for the other team,
They're just runners up!

Gary McFall (12)
Gleniffer High School

SOMEONE SPECIAL

Do you have someone special?
Who makes you laugh and never cry,
Makes you feel warm inside
And is always there and never says bye?

Even if they're in your heart
You love them even more.
To me that is the one I can trust,
And the one I adore.

Karen Palmer (11)
Gleniffer High School

HALLOWE'EN

Candy bags and sweets
Chocolatey treats.
Scary faces,
And spooky places.
Horrible jokes
Which will scare the old folks.
So, beware!
Hallowe'en is here!

Denise Farmer (12)
Gleniffer High School

CHRISTMAS

C   hristmas is about
H   appy children
R   ushing
I   n and out
S   hops, buying
T   oys for friends
M   arvellous
A   ngels
S   inging praise to God.

Rebecca McKay (12)
Gleniffer High School

MY PAPA

Papa, Dad, Husband, Brother,
He was a great man.
I'm sure of that.
I know I am.
He loved my gran.
He loved her lots and lots.
He always talked about my mum,
- Aunt Leslie and Uncle Cameron.
He loved them too.
They loved him back

Oh Westies! His face would
light up when he saw 'Haggis' -
'Coorie' as well - he talked
about him lots
all the time

He didn't like Cheri being away
He loved us too

Glasgow Rangers. That's papa alright
If we went past 'Ibrox' he would shout
'The Hall of Science!'

He told us how much
Aunt Isobel cared for him

He made all those toys
How did he do it?

That's Wallace.

Karrie Reilly (12)
Gleniffer High School

LONELINESS KNOWS US

Loneliness is everything we fear,
it swallows us whole and it takes us
into a deep hole of endless sadness
that we can't escape from.
Loneliness eats away at our thoughts
and cherished memories of true love.
It poisons our minds and souls.
Loneliness knows our fears and inadequacies
that we'll run and fall apart in tears of pain,
although we shed crystal tears of fear we are
brave and unafraid of loneliness for our minds
and souls are free in this small but large world
of dishonesty and false intentions.

Leighann Anderson (17)
Gleniffer High School

AUTUMN LEAVES

Leaves are falling off the trees,
Swaying gently in the breeze.
When the children hurry around,
the leaves get crumpled to the ground.
The colours of which are quite amazing,
Brown, yellow and red are all really glazing.
When winter comes in a steady pace,
The leaves disappear without a trace.

Ryan Miller (11)
Gleniffer High School

FOOTBALL

F   ootball is cool
O   n the field you get a great feeling
O   ff the field watching it is even better
T   he footie grounds have a great feeling singing and shouting
B   ut most of all I like to score a goal
A   t half-time we have a drink and a team talk
L   aughter and shouting when the goals are scored.
L   ast of all we looovvvveee to see our team win.

John Allison (11)
Gleniffer High School

CHRISTMAS

Christmas time is nearly here
Everyone's excited.
No one sheds a tear
As they are all delighted.

The shops are always busy
Some people get quite mad
Some even get quite dizzy,
But in the end everyone's glad
    It's Christmas.

Samantha Barr (11)
Gleniffer High School

CHRISTMAS

C arol singers in the street below
H ear them sing before they go
R udolph's nose's shining bright
I nto the sky he takes his flight
S now lies on the ground outside
T oddlers jump up and down
M istletoe held above our heads,
    time to kiss and wish the best.
A fter all Santa's been and gone
S o it's time to think of the year ahead.

Stacey Smith (12)
Gleniffer High School

AMERICA

Americans crying
People are dying
Around we are stunned
Our senses are numbed.

The people cry war
Others wonder what for
The killing is senseless
Leaves us feeling defenceless.

Natalie Wright (13)
Gleniffer High School

WAR

I hear the cries and screams of small, bewildered children searching high and low for any traces of their families.

Walking down this road of a ghost town, I imagine what it would be like to live here at a time like this.

People are lying in the gutter, tugging at my leg to ask me the same question 'Do you know where my home is?' I can't answer though as I don't know where I am.

Looking up I see loved ones jumping out of skyscrapers and office buildings, hoping to survive together if not to die in each others arms at least.

Families everywhere look for any relation to them but have no hope of knowing if they are alive or dead.

There may be survival under the rubble but anyone thinking this will have to keep wondering in the meantime.

Then I see a little boy with a whimpering pussy cat on his lap who has lost its tail through it all. Cuddling it, he is telling the creature through tears running down his face that everything will be fine and that they will get through this together, that's when I realise that this is no nightmare, it is all true and this is my home. My country is at the dreaded war.

That's when I see my mum's ring in the dust and her face beside it.

All that I have left is memories and I ask myself one thing, 'Is there any point in living?'

Laura Walker (12)
Hamilton Grammar School

11TH SEPTEMBER 2001

The heat, the smoke
Burning my throat.
At every turn
People scream, choke, pray and die.
A child, barely four years old, cries
Nobody listens.
All in a blind panic,
The flames,
Too close.
The stairs, blocked,
The elevator, jammed,
People trapped,
Gasping for breath, screaming for mercy.
The stagnant smell
Of sweat, blood and death.
There's nothing I can do
Nothing anyone can do,
But wait, hope for help
If it ever comes.
What happened to the land of dreams, of plenty?
I guess I'll never know in this life,
The one that flashes before me.
So many people, yet I feel so alone
Such a waste
Men, women, children,
Just starting out.
I look for answers,
The one thing I know for sure;
I'm not getting out of here alive.
9:52am.

Laura Moodley (14)
Hamilton Grammar School

IT'S A RAINY DAY

The doors are closed and there is nothing to do
I hear the pitter-patter on the window sill
All the jigsaws have been done and put away
The prickly, cold, blue carpet jags into my legs,
While my eyes hurt at the sight of the plain, white, same-old walls,
It's a rainy day and there's nothing to do!

I'm all dressed up but have nowhere to go
I'm sick of listening to the same music,
Watching the same old videos,
And doing the same old thing,
It's a rainy day and there's nothing to do!

I hear the humming of the fridge,
I taste the empty taste of nothing inside my mouth,
I smell the large layer of dust on the mantelpiece,
I see the rain running down the outside of the window
And the dry, unopened umbrella, sitting on the bed.
I am bored because
It's a rainy day and there's nothing to do!

Lorna Scoular (12)
Hamilton Grammar School

THE BIGGEST FLOOD OF THE YEAR

Waves were crashing,
Cliffs were trembling
With the force of water.
The lighthouse was flashing,
The ships were rocking,
The wind blowing slates off the roof.

It was raining hard
The roads were flooded,
The drains were blocked.
Rubber dinghies were floating
Up the road.

All the children were hiding
The thunder and lightning started,
Rumble, crash.
Light poles were tumbling down
There was a power cut.

Then the houses got flooded
Everybody slept upstairs.

The fire brigade came next day
To unblock the drains,
The sea is calm again.

But there is still a flood,
The roads are still blocked,
Because of the light poles.

It is the biggest flood of the year.

Richard McColl (14)
Hillside School

I WILL NEVER UNDERSTAND

People that believe in star signs,
I don't understand
How can they read that gibberish
Is what I want to know?
They are not just in the paper,
They are in magazines too
You can even have them sent to your mobile phone.
If I was writing in,
To the reader I would make it clear,
Get a life and stop believing horoscopes
Here,
But no matter how hard I try,
Why people read star signs
I will never understand.

John Malcolm (11)
Holy Cross High School

VIRGO

Virgo a perfectionist
Never wrong,
Girl of the zodiac
Colour co-ordinated
Everything always matches whether it is
Hats, shoes, handbags and clothes
Never, ever seen in jogging trousers.

Susan Studders (12)
Holy Cross High School

THE REAL ZODIACS

Today the Scorpio will be happy,
Something good will be in store,
Just remember to not be snappy,
As a tall, dark stranger is going to walk straight through your door.

Tomorrow there will be storm clouds,
Gathering in your living room,
Watch out Libra there might be rows,
Just hide away and stay away from crowds.

Capricorns are usually fearful,
Aquarians are usually tearful,
Taurians are surprisingly gleeful,
Where as Geminis are terribly pitiful,
Arians are remarkably crazy,
Cancerians are known to be lazy,
Virgoans are always early,
Sagittarians are usually late,
But they'll both be on time if they've got a smashing date.
Pisceans like more than just one friend,
But Leos will stick by you until the very end.

Jenna Kelly (11)
Holy Cross High School

A PISCEAN IS COOL TO BE

A Piscean is cool to be
You're wise for your wisdom to help you,
And other people know what is right and wrong,
Kind to give your help and support it to your classmates,
Intelligent, you always know the right thing to say to people,
So being a Piscean is cool!

Kirstie McGurk (12)
Holy Cross High School

TRUE PISCEAN

Piscean girls, you may think they're sweet,
But are you sure this is the star sign you'd like to meet?

You might think they're quite quiet
Would you think that when they start a riot?
See a Piscean in a trance, you may think she's a dreamy girl
Actually they're making their plans to take over the world.

You might think a boy band is their music fave
But to loud rock music they'd rather rave
You think they'd be good girls, go the right way
Watch out or it'll be Pisceans that lead you astray.

Piscean girls are meant to be romantic, sensitive,
I'll assure you that fact is a myth!
You'd think that Piscean girls would be generous with their time
In fact, they'd like to be on their own, just fine.

You'd think that Pisceans would like to be with their family, right?
Rubbish! They'd much rather be out, taking part in a gang fight
You'd think that Piscean girls are as cute, quiet and sweet as mice,
Read my poem, this is the true Pisceans!

Piscean girls may look as though they are in a dream,
Be careful! They're not as nice as they seem . . .

Kerry Anne Callaghan (12)
Holy Cross High School

MISS SAGITTARIUS

When you're fit and ambitious,
Completely bootilicious,
Cool and kind
Have a very sensitive mind,
Then you are definitely Sagittarian.

If you wear a lot of lippy,
Prefer to have things nippy,
Forever and always working,
If you never, ever stop smirking,
Then you're born to be Sagittarian.

Katie O'Hanlon (11)
Holy Cross High School

WHO CARES ABOUT THE FUTURE?

You'll find it in the newspaper,
Or on the Internet,
If something bad is supposed to happen,
You begin to fret.

You bought a book on it,
You read it every day,
Come on, just admit it,
It's driving you crazy.

Who cares about the future?
I don't see why you do,
You and stupid horoscopes
It just doesn't seem like you.

Then something wonderful happens,
That you had never read,
Suddenly you realise
You had been mislead.

You come crawling back to me
As if nothing ever happened,
But I stand, arms wide open,
You are still my friend.

Daria Di Mambro (11)
Holy Cross High School

CAPRICORN SUPERSTAR

C apricorn is earning mega bucks as an executive
A little over cautious!
P retty and stylish
R uns for January sales
I ntelligent worker
C ool designer
O beys all the rules to be very smart
R eally tough and determined
N ow you have read the poems, that's how to be a Capricorn.

Danielle Neilson (11)
Holy Cross High School

BOSSY, BOSSY, BIG-HEADED LEO

Bossy, bossy, big-headed Leo
Yap, yap, yap, yap, yap, yap
Fancy dress
And hair all a mess.
Up all night
First to sing on the karaoke
Last to fall into bed that night
Six inch heels
And spike nails.
Bossy, bossy, big-headed Leo.

Stephanie Murphy (12)
Holy Cross High School

SUBMARINE SPECTRUM

Neptune's feast invites to tropics
Lavish, clear and sunlit sea
Walnut widens to brain coral
Spectrum swirls on zigzag mail.

Sulphur fins the sapphire bodies
Orange spotting sage-green flank
Peacock rims the chocolate scales
Golden tails glint arrow's aim.

Swarming, darting, courting always
With stripes, dots, patches, eye-spots
They quiver agleam and battle,
Flexing their bull fighter's capes.

Colm Macqueen (14)
Largs Academy

WHAT IS LOVE?

Love is a strong emotion
That you feel when the time is right
It's some kind of spell-binding potion
That makes you want to hold on tight.

For if you lose that love
You can experience a frightening fall
But then you ask yourself
Was it really love at all?

Ashley Simpson (15)
Larkhall Academy

ANGER

The hot air is stifling
Breathing is as awkward as that
Of a shuddering volcano,
Built up and boiling over,
Spewing scorching lava over the helpless
Victims below
Unstoppable and unmerciful.

Suddenly a cool breeze blows and the flow
Slows to a halt
A rain of apologies follows which
Falls on burnt, tarred ears
Which listen but do not hear.

The debris is cleared, but a separation creeps in
Fear builds a solid concrete wall.

Michelle Little (16)
Larkhall Academy

TRYING TO FORGET

Am I supposed to just forget it,
Forget how I feel?
Just forget everything that was said
How can I forget the lies?
Forget the wanting,
I thought it was real
   . . . just forget it.

Lindsey Thomson (15)
Larkhall Academy

IT'S YOU I SEE

It's you I see
Staring into the depths of my soul
Enquiring eyes, wandering over me
Willing me, climb into the abyssful black hole
For it's you and the reality only you can see.

It's you I see
Knowing that my smile is fake
Seeing that my laughter isn't true
Being aware of the goals I cannot make
While all the time relying on you.

It's you I see,
I cannot escape your resentful glare
That look of disgust, distaste
Crushing my confidence with your stare
I know it's true - I'm a waste.

It's you I see
Telling me things I do not want to hear,
'You're stupid! You're fat! You're ugly!'
A failure. Confirmation of my greatest fear
Whilst you there, smiling smugly.

It's you I see
I cannot run, I cannot hide
You'll get me, you always do
Searching, searching deep inside
Leave me alone, I hate you!

It's me you see,
In the mirror, staring out
It's myself I'm destroying, I see
My own reflection, filled with doubt
My own worst enemy is me.

Laura Telfer (16)
Larkhall Academy

REALISATION

I sit and watch you, watching me
As I gaze hopefully into your loving eyes
Wondering when our lips will touch again
I realise . . .

When we quarrel I feel your hurt,
When those innocent tears fall down your soft, gentle face,
As I move them away
I realise . . .

As we part at night, I feel helpless
My heart aches for your return
Every second feels like an hour
Time goes on so long
I realise you are the one.

Lauren Craig (16)
Larkhall Academy

STUPIDITY

I may be bird-brained, but not stupid,
I may be bone-headed, but not stupid,
I may be brainless, but not stupid,
I may be clueless, but not stupid,
I may be dopey, but not stupid,
I may be feather-brained, but not stupid,
I may be feeble-minded, but not stupid,
I'm not stupid, just uneducated.

Sandy Nicol (15)
Larkhall Academy

HATE

You taste that bitter taste,
You taste that sharp,
Biting, bitter taste,
Your heart beats hard in your ears,
Loud and hard.
The black cloud envelops you
Covers your eyes,
All you see,
All you see,
All you feel,
All you know,
Is hate.
Hard hate,
Angry hate,
Terrible hate,
Everlasting hate.

Jade Rodger (15)
Larkhall Academy

AUTHORITY

That feeling inside you,
That sharp, digging feeling,
The oppression,
It will always be there,
It will never leave you,
It will always rule you.

Matthew Wadsworth (16)
Larkhall Academy

OUR FOUR SENSES

Without my sight, I cannot see
The beauties of this world
I cannot see the silky, blue sky
Everything I see is a blur.

Without my hearing, I cannot hear
The sound of music from out there
I cannot hear a sweet, sweet voice
Only a slight, slight echo in my ear.

Without my touch, I cannot feel
What I have never felt before
The softness of a teddy bear
I will never know again.

Without my sense of smell
I cannot experience those
The smell of flowers in a field
I will never know again.

Natalie Sorbie (16)
Larkhall Academy

WAR

Like rotten plums
Cold and damp.
Burning, raging fires,
Death and hatred.
Shouting, firing guns and blasting bombs,
All because of two people who believe differently.
War, horrible war.

Laura Smith (14)
Larkhall Academy

ALONE

As I sit here, all alone,
My eyes are red from crying
I try to forget
But my hope is dying.

I close my eyes
The thoughts remain
I can't escape them
They cause me so much pain.

I can't look at my reflection,
All I see is a tear
I can't look at my expression
All I see is fear.

Why doesn't anyone understand
What's going on inside?
They never see the real me,
I always have to hide.

Life goes on,
Or so they say
But I have no choice,
They make me stay.

The pain is nearly over now
Although some will not go
It's such a shame
That life can get this low.

The tears have stopped
There's nothing left to say
But this won't be the last
Tomorrow's another day.

Amanda Perrow (15)
Larkhall Academy

THE RACIST

Why are you always calling me names
Leaving me out of your fun and games?
Just because I have darker skin
You treat me as though I belong in the bin.
There's not much difference between me and you
If you were to cut me I would bleed too.
You have a family, a sister and two brothers,
Do you treat them the way you treat others?
You always act so big and tough
Stomping around and being so rough.
Name calling is not what I do
'Cause I'm not a bully, unlike you.
But it will be your turn, just you wait
Then you won't act so big and great.
So calling me names I will just ignore
'Cause to everyone it's becoming a bore.

Derek McDonald (15)
Larkhall Academy

FRIENDSHIP

Friendship
So many things to me
Happy, sometimes sad it can make us be.
Without it we'd be lost
Yet sometimes we pay a cost
As comforting as the sound of winter rain
Battering off my window as I lie in bed
To feel as safe as when your mother tucks you in as a child
A helping hand they always lend
All these feelings we long for in a friend.

Alison Mackenzie (16)
Larkhall Academy

NEW

To live,
Acting on impulse,
Foul play,
All those sacrifices,
Hope she noticed,
Speechless at,
How you feel.

Everything's different,
But exactly the same,
Burning a candle,
To hide the darkness with the flame,
Uncoordinated, unsophisticated,
Eyes right,
Head down.

I'm seeing red,
Pretending doesn't stop the pain,
Dancing won't ease the strain,
Poisoned ivy,
May be,
But I have,
Life goes on,
Unfortunately?
Prise my heart from your grip,
Brutal distraction,
Escape to reality,
Killer fish,
Trial hard,
Made it,
But left your soul.

Laura Gibson (16)
Larkhall Academy

REVENGE

Revenge,
Revenge,
The bitterness turned so sweet
Changing to anger the sorrow we shall meet.

Revenge,
Revenge,
From which poems and plays are written
Like the attack from a dog, we are bitten.

Revenge,
Revenge,
The supposed repair to all our sadness,
Although only submerging us in total madness.

Revenge,
Revenge,
The pain it does not remove
For this is the only thing, that it shall improve.

Graham Smith (16)
Larkhall Academy

HOLIDAYS

H   olidays are good,
O   nly sunshine and sand
L   ie in on the holidays
I   don't have any homework
D   ays are long and warm
A   lways fun and happy
Y   ou and your friends can hang out
S   unshine all day long.

John Wadsworth (14)
Larkhall Academy

THE STREET

Small, short steps,
Plodding into town
Dimly lit by twinkling amber lights
The quiet street.

Sharp, silver shutters
Cover all the crumbling doors
With grubby ancient shop fronts
The obsolete street.

Strong, stale smells
Blowing in the wind
While litter floats along the gutter
The uninviting street.

Philip Speedie (16)
Larkhall Academy

UNDERSTANDING

I don't understand
Why people fight over petty little things
Such as the music to listen to
Or the video to watch
But most of all
You've got to realise one thing
People have different tastes
What I understand most is
Each individual is a human being
And has a right to their own choice!

Jayne Fleming (13)
Larkhall Academy

BEST FRIEND

Almost everyone has a best friend
They are the people you can trust most in the world
And you expect them not to tell your secrets.

Best friends don't look identical
That's what makes it perfect.
You are two different people who have the same interests
Like boys, clothes and music
But you can be completely different,
One can like going to discos
Going shopping all the time
And going out almost every night.

And the other can like sleepovers,
Hanging out and going shopping sometimes.

Best friends should have a really strong bond
And nothing should be able to break it.

Lots of people will have five or six best friends in a lifetime
But sooner or later there will be one that is extra special
And maybe, just maybe
They will be the best friend of all.

Carol Graham (14)
Larkhall Academy

ON THE OUTSIDE

On the outside of the walls which surround me
On the outside is the freedom I crave
When I'm there I'll be so free
When I'm there my soul you'll save.

Scott Smith (16)
Larkhall Academy

LOST

As I feel a trickle running down my face
It really is hot here
Where am I? I just want to go home
As I daze into a dream world
I'm all alone.

I can taste salty water, oh it's just sweat
All I can see is an open space
What is this place?

Could it get any worse?
I shouldn't have said that
I need a drink,
I start seeing things
I can't even think.

I fall to my knees, angry and shattered
Somebody help!
I see a figure in the distance, beyond a heatwave
I run towards him but he doesn't exist
I am lost!

Kristoffer Corbett (13)
Larkhall Academy

ANGER

Anger is like pepper on your tongue
Like a thousand knives stabbing you all over your body
The ghastly smell of bins and rubbish
Like thunder and lightning in the dark, night sky
The constant ringing in my ears.

Laura Thomson (14)
Larkhall Academy

DREAMS

D   aydreams in class,
R   eally do come true,
E   very night I dream too.
A   s I lie upon my bed
M   y thoughts go round and round my head
S   nuggle time, go to bed, sleepy time for me and ted.

Rhona Lees (14)
Larkhall Academy

LOVE

Love is the smile on my lover's face,
The smell of his aftershave as he holds me close,
The sweetness of candy,
His soft, lingering kisses,
And when I hear our song,
It reminds me of the long summer.
Love gives me life.

Claire Hamilton (14)
Larkhall Academy

LIFE IS . . .

War is the anger inside,
Fear is the darkness of the night,
Hatred is the green in our eyes,
Death is the sadness we feel,
Love is the beat of your heart,
Life is the puzzle nobody can solve.

Lynsay Rennie (14)
Larkhall Academy

HAPPINESS

Feels like silk or velvet,
Smells like flowers, red roses or tulips,
Just like the taste of a big chocolate cake
Or a love song sang softly,
A little fluffy kitten pure white and tame.
Happiness is all of these things and more
Rolled into one emotion.

Gayle Loggie (14)
Larkhall Academy

CLOUDS

Clouds are candyfloss
Which feel like a fluffy pillow.
They remind me of cotton wool,
Angel Delight in the sky
Sounds like the sea on a windy day.

Linsey Sneddon (14)
Larkhall Academy

FEAR

Blood in your mouth,
Thunder in your ear,
Lightning in your eyes,
Cold water on your back,
Burnt rubber passing by your nose.

Fear makes me scared.

Graeme Smith (13)
Larkhall Academy

WAR

Awaiting the battle, all is silent
But soon it will be violent
Soldiers are praying for loved ones
Before they ply their guns.
On the plane, the atmosphere is cold
Like stories past generations have told.
Then through the sky they plunge
Landing on the squelchy battlefield which feels like gunge.
Now all they have to do is wait
For God to decide their fate.

Laura Dyer (14)
Larkhall Academy

FROST

Frost is a powerful thing
It clings to you like a wet blanket.
Covering everything that dares to cross its path,
It seeps through flowing rivers and trickling streams.
Sometimes it acts invisible,
Blind to the human eye,
Causing you to slip and slide like a newborn calf
But then the sun reappears,
Making frost cower away in fear.
The sun is the hero again . . .
. . . until next time.

Alison King (14)
Larkhall Academy

SCOTTISH WATER

Falls from the sky
Isn't very shy.
Hits the ground
Never to be found.
Some escapes and rotates
Into the deep depths of the reservoir.
Only to come out, nice and clean
Getting ready for the big machine.
All is pure and chemically fresh
While travelling along the dark, twisty pipes.
The end is complete
When summoned, jets out
Waiting to be consumed by the mouth.

Gareth Kerr (14)
Larkhall Academy

CLOUDS

Clouds are like ice cream,
Sweet vanilla to be exact
They're like a lovely white poodle,
Like just-baked bread,
Just like sweet music.
A lullaby, a love song.
Cotton wool balls floating in the sky,
Soft and fluffy,
Harmless until turned black and heavy
By the storm.

Jenna Smith (14)
Larkhall Academy

UNITED

On September 11th 2001 the world stood still,
As millions of people got a sudden chill.

Bin Laden was the man behind the attack,
And now the allies are determined to fight back.

George Bush said Britain was America's true friend,
And it's now time to bring terrorism to an end.

The famous Twin Towers crumbled that day,
Just because a man couldn't get his own way.

Imagine being in those planes up in the sky,
When you find out that you will soon die.

Everybody from all over the place,
Pulled people from under the Twin Tower disgrace.

The question is, will he do it again?
If he does his life will be brought to an end.

The Taliban have declared a holy war
And for the allies there is everything to fight for.

Bin Laden must be one sick guy,
If he is willing to let all those innocent people die.

Dead or alive is the way he is wanted,
But will New York be forever haunted?

I can't imagine what some families are going through,
They probably say 'Bin Laden, we hate you'.

It makes you wonder why there are people like him,
People that do nothing but cause a great sin.

It is good to see countries stand together,
To end Bin Laden's reign of terror.

It was a day that no one will forget in a hurry,
But now it is time for Bin Laden to worry.

David Hogg (14)
Larkhall Academy

LAST FEW DAYS

Don't take things for granted
Look after what you've got
We just keep wanting more
Though we've got an awful lot.
Genetically modified organisms, petrol and hair spray.
Use these and the world may be living its last few days.
Ultraviolet rays destroy the ozone layer,
Look after your environment
Show the world you care,
Where will we go if the world comes to a halt?
Well there is nowhere else and it'll be all our fault!

Yvonne Jewkes (14)
Larkhall Academy

DEATH

D arkness
E nd of life
A fterlife
T ime to go
H eaven.

Jill Graham (14)
Larkhall Academy

CHOCOLATE

A soft, creamy taste,
Yet it feels hard to touch.
It has a fear, a fear of being torn apart,
Eaten or broken into pieces.
The warmth of being melted,
A luxury smell to my nose
The sound of rustling, shiny paper.
They cover my eyes,
Those large, brown squares.

Charlene McInally (14)
Larkhall Academy

STUPIDITY

Clowns fooling around in the circus,
High-pitched laughter,
Rough toilet paper,
Sour lemons,
Fire blazing and smouldering away.

Stupidity makes me feel foolish.

Arianne Fox (13)
Larkhall Academy

FRIENDSHIP

People talking to each other,
Smells like chocolate and fresh flowers,
Soft, smooth, silky,
Talking kindly to each other,
Tastes like candy apples.

Danielle Scott (11)
Larkhall Academy

FEAR

Death itself
A drop of ice-cold water running down your back,
Blood in your mouth,
A burning fire,
Someone screaming as death falls upon them.
I hope I will never have to experience it.

Iain Walker (13)
Larkhall Academy

FEAR

A cold, dark, frosty night,
A dark, dark creepy forest with wolves howling,
A smelly, blazing fire,
Sounds like someone screaming nearby,
Tastes like burnt toast.

Fear makes me feel terrified.

Rachel Simpson (13)
Larkhall Academy

SADNESS

Rotting waste at a dump,
People crying their eyes out,
Sour milk in your mouth,
A dying figure in pain,
Someone has been murdered,
Sadness makes me scream!

Lynsey Douglas (12)
Larkhall Academy

PEACE

Strawberries and cream melting in my mouth,
Toffee and caramel aroma twirling round in circles,
A relaxing feeling like sitting on a huge, furry throne,
Soft, twirling waves on the beach,
Curling blue and purple with yellow, smily faces looking at me,
Peace makes me feel calm.

Jane McLaren (12)
Larkhall Academy

FEAR

A strange looking man in a long, dark coat following me,
A cold, frosty morning,
A bitter lemon in your mouth,
A painful scream,
Sour milk and rotten garbage.

Fear makes me feel cold inside.

Stephanie Steele (12)
Larkhall Academy

FEAR

Looking in a dark alley,
A shiver running down your spine,
Tastes like sour milk,
Smells like burning rubber,
Like nails scraping down the blackboard.

Fear makes me feel terrified.

Claire Hamilton (13)
Larkhall Academy

FEAR

A scary man walking down the dark street,
With a knife with blood dripping off it.
The feel of a knife ready to go through you,
Roasting hot strawberries in your mouth,
A cremated man,
The sound of someone screaming when the knife is going through them.

Fear makes me scared to go anywhere by myself.

Andrea McAulay (12)
Larkhall Academy

STUPIDITY

Like someone with shoes on the wrong feet,
Someone tickling me under my arm,
Sweets with a weird and funny name,
Like my mum mixing two recipes together,
Someone giggling at something that isn't funny.

Stupidity makes me laugh till I cry.

Andrew Marshall (13)
Larkhall Academy

PEACE

A calm, warm day
With birds singing,
A sweet smell of daisies.
It tastes thick and creamy.
Feels like soft, thin silk.

Lisa Dyer (12)
Larkhall Academy

FRIENDSHIP

It feels like hot tea, cuddly toys, soft pillows and a warm sun,
Chocolate, strawberries and cream, hot chocolate,
A red, pink and yellow room with a cute puppy in the centre.
Smells of flowers and the scent of a new candle.
It sounds like sweet music, birds chirping
And your best friend calling on you to come.

Fiona Tennant (11)
Larkhall Academy

WHAT IS STUPIDITY?

Someone walking around with pants on their head,
Having a plate of curry and ice cream,
A bucket of cold beans being poured over you,
My friend laughing her head off,
Perfume and aftershave mixed together.

Stupidity makes me feel as if
I am going to explode inside with laughter.

Emma Smith (13)
Larkhall Academy

STUPIDITY

The silly cat tripping over the mat,
A bath full of beans,
Chips in chocolate sauce,
Shampoo mixed with vinegar,
A clown dying of laughter.

Stupidity makes me jump with joy.

David Morrison (12)
Larkhall Academy

FEAR

A man in a dark street alone with you.

A thud is pounding the inside of my body.

I have a taste of rotten, burnt toast.

I can smell mouldy boiled eggs.

I can hear drips right next to me.

Fear makes me tremble.

Aaron Wark (12)
Larkhall Academy

PEACE

A black man and a white man shaking hands.

Like silk in my hand.

Vanilla ice cream in your mouth.

Flowers blooming in spring.

Birds singing in the trees.

Greig Hawke (13)
Larkhall Academy

HAPPINESS

A child's smile lights up the room,
Tastes like hot, melting chocolate.
Smells like daffodils growing in the garden,
The music of the choir singing in the background.

Graeme Sorbie (12)
Larkhall Academy

FRIENDSHIP

It sounds like children playing in a park
and tastes like fresh baked bread.
Children playing like nice ice cream.
It smells like a fruit flower
and the touch of a new bike.
It's called friendship.

Jayson M Duncan (12)
Larkhall Academy

HAPPINESS

A cute, little puppy rubbing his tummy
Warm, soft and silky,
Melted chocolate, ice cream, yummy.
Strong beautiful roses
And children giggle and hearts tighten.

Natalie Vance (12)
Larkhall Academy

FEAR

A horror film that scares children,
It feels sharp and bristly,
Strong, spicy, slimy,
It smells like raw meat,
The sound of people screaming and shouting.

Scott Paton (12)
Larkhall Academy

FEAR

Looks like a man dressed in black,
Walking down an alleyway,
It tastes like a burnt pizza,
Feels like frozen ice,
Things burning in a fire.
Sounds like people screaming and shouting.

Kim Graham (12)
Larkhall Academy

STUPIDITY

Billy Connolly joking about,
Like ice cream melting all over your hand,
Barbecued Jaffa Cakes tingling your taste buds,
Cremated sticky toffee pudding,
Children laughing at the circus.

Stupidity makes me giggle.

Lesley Ballantyne (13)
Larkhall Academy

PEACE

An extremely still lake with no one around,
You're falling onto a soft cloud,
Ice cream slowly melting in your mouth,
The nice, fresh, clean air.
Sounds like nothing at all.

Peace makes me feel tranquil.

Salaam Ahmad (13)
Larkhall Academy

FEAR

Death and fire,
Citric acid in your mouth,
Walking down a dark street,
A cold, wet knife going down your back,
Fire and blood.

Fear makes me feel scared.

Alison Campbell (12)
Larkhall Academy

PRISON

Four prison walls,
Surrounding me,
Engulfing me,
But I must not think,
For thought is the enemy.

Four prison walls,
Huge, grey and dark,
The bare cell; empty,
But I must not think,
For thought leads to insanity.

Four prison walls,
A tiny tray of food,
Just enough to live on,
But I must not think,
For thought is the enemy.

Four prison walls,
A tiny barred window,
I wonder what's outside . . .

Josh Coats (11)
Lomond School

THE PRISONER

Alone in the darkness
This inky, black cavity
Hopes to suppress
My feelings of optimism.

Alone in the darkness,
This dismal, black hole,
Separates me from love
And leaves me desolate.

Alone in the darkness
My mind allows me to anticipate
Survival, freedom, comfort,
In a new life ahead.

Alone in the darkness
My keen senses pick up on
The foul stench of suffering
In other enclosures.

Alone in the darkness
I feel the coldness of the floor
Chill me to the bone.
I fumble around to find warmth.

Alone in the darkness
I hear the guards' footsteps
And grating voices
Pierce through the gloom.

Out of the darkness
A seed of thought begins to grow.
An escape plan develops
And hope is not lost.

Jonathan McLatchie (12)
Lomond School

KITE

She threw me up into the cloudy sky
The forest became a smudge of green,
And the hills nearby.

I danced beautifully,
With my colours gleaming,
High in the sky
I could fly!

The cord snapped,
And I was whisked away,
By the wind driving me,
Far away into the night's sky.

I raced along the skyline,
With my tail near by,
Waggling along,
Like a dog on a high.

But, bang, crash, thump, dump
I landed in the fresh grass,
My flight had ended,
And I was dead, lying lifeless.

Laura McHard (12)
Lomond School

JOURNEY

I entered a field made colourful by the great sheets of canvas
The heat was immense as they began to fill the balloons
I got in and looked around the vast expanse of colours
And shapes as the balloons slowly left the ground.

Once we were high enough we were picked up by an
Arm of wind and carried over towns and villages where
The people were ruled by gravity.
We passed through immense sheets of white and grey
To find the everlasting golden glow of the sun.

Robert Stevenson (14)
Lomond School

IMPRISONMENT

Scared, lonely and trapped
Was how I felt inside my prison cell.
I hated it - waking up every morning
In my dark, damp cage.

Every day was the same,
Inside the prison camp.
Wake up, get given scraps of food
And then sleep.

The camp was a living hell
Dark, dingy and dreary
You could taste dust from
The stony paths.
Prisoners died of illness, beatings
And many more dreadful things
That occurred in the camp.

In my bed I would think
How cruel the pain was.
Telling myself one day
I would be free.

Robbie Liddell (12)
Lomond School

Journey To Paradise

I step on the plane
My briefcase under one arm
The time is so precious
Is it a journey to remember
Or a journey like any other?
The journey end is in sight.

Engines throw us above the clouds
Is this Heaven?
Am I dreaming?
Relaxing in my cramped armchair
Looking through my porthole to the world outside
The journey end is in sight.

Announcements show that progress is well
Still I return to my restless position
Constant chatter
Sudden bleeps
When will this end?
The journey end is in sight.

Suddenly awoken
Alarm bells ringing
What is happening?
Movement and muffled words leave me shaken
A flow of people race to the tail
I'm pushed to join them
The journey end is in sight.

Silence is now the main element
Dictated by others with shining blades
I'm afraid
Beads of sweat
Where are we going?
What will happen?
Altitude quickly decreases
The journey end is in sight.

My ears pop
My stomach is in my mouth
Pushed next to the door's window
I see fast-approaching land
A huge city
We're too low
Buildings flash past
Two stand in our way
One is at point-blank
Bright light
The journey end is in sight.

Greig Logan (14)
Lomond School

THE HOUSE MARTIN

You sit in that lonely evergreen branch
Wings folded, resting only your head moving,
Looking and waiting for the moment,
Your journey is to begin again.

You lie in wait for the rest of them,
Your head twitching wanting to go,
Far away from the bitter north
Into the warm climate of the south.

As you set off your feathers are ruffled,
By the chilly October winds.
You know that winter's presence is near
And its path is not a friendly one.

Sailing through the sunset sky,
You glide with others,
I hope you make that travel to the south
Take flight little bird, goodbye.

Rebecca Stephenson (12)
Lomond School

GETTING READY FOR SCHOOL

I get up in the morning
I feel sick and tired,
I've got my exams today,
I have to be wired.

I get my breakfast,
Fix my tie,
Then I ask myself,
Why, why, why?

I walk over the hills and round the bends,
Like I said, it never ends.

I finally get there,
I walked the whole way;
But then I realise, it's Saturday!

Craig Kelly (12)
Lomond School

JOURNEY OF TERROR

Three flights, just like normal, just a basic routine.
Three flights, millions of restless nights.

One moment of shock, as a nation takes an almighty knock,
One minute of silence, an eternity of disbelief,
And everlasting sadness, mourning and grief.

Collapsing of world famous buildings,
Collapsing of morals,
Collapsing of world famous society.

Three journeys of terror on the 11th of September
We shall all remember.

Christopher Donnachie (14)
Lomond School

THE JOURNEY

It rumbled loudly
Vibrating under our feet
The over-stuffed chairs
Spewed out fluff
The 'No smoking' signs were ignored
As people blew smoke into our faces
The rubbish on the tacky floor
Crackled and crunched beneath us.
The air was filled with irritating sounds
The sniffing of noses, continuous coughing
The atmosphere was tense
As the carriage occupants
Waited impatiently
For their
Destined
Stop.

Anna Dobson (11)
Lomond School

ROLLER COASTER RIDE

My legs were shaking with fear as I waited in the long queue,
The time was passing so quickly,
Before I knew, my carriage awaited me,
As I stepped into it my fear passed and I was filled with excitement,
I went up, up to the peak,
I closed my eyes tightly,
All my thoughts were unthinkable as I flew down the windy track,
Suddenly . . . jerk! I had come to a halt;
My journey had finished,
I ran to the end of the line to begin my journey again!

Caroline Wylie (12)
Lomond School

A JOURNEY THROUGH THE SEASONS

As the world awakens from a long sleep,
Happiness and warmth enlightens everyone,
As each individual lamb is born,
Another daffodil flowers,
Bringing joy into everyone's heart
Birds sing delightful songs,
Whilst the trees overwhelm themselves with leaves,
One bumblebee is spotted, then two,
Within a matter of weeks,
Bees are flying from flower to flower collecting pollen.

As the warm breeze becomes warmer,
And the grass becomes greener,
The waters begin to shimmer in the air of summer,
The deep, blue skies are never faulted with a cloud,
Whilst the burning sun bakes above everyone,
The world, once again, is filled with laughter and smiles
As enthusiasm grows,
The constant, harsh hit of a tennis ball is heard,
Whilst passion rises - lovers watch the sunset late at night,
And a glowing, friendly atmosphere is created,
The birds continue to sing with a graceful everlasting sound which
Enchants people as it never fades.

A chill fills the evening air
Turning leaves golden brown
As the final few birds attempt to sing as lively as ever,
Gradually the winds encourage the crispy leaves to fall,
Whilst Hallowe'en and Guy Fawkes' night welcome winter,
And more darkness and bleak, icy weather.
Within weeks, the weather dramatically becomes colder,
And the last few leaves have been rid of,
A spiritless and motionless atmosphere hovers around
As many animals go into hibernation,
By the time January has arrived, temperatures decline to their
                                        most coldest

The skies are no longer cloudless but overcast,
Inside many houses blazing fire roar for warmth
The next few months are to be depressing and disheartening
But life will still re-awaken in spring.

Kara Dawson (12)
Lomond School

JOURNEYS

To journey through time
Would be just great
You could see what happened
On a particular date.

If I was to journey
Through history
Where would I go?
That's the mystery.

I'd visit the Romans,
And visit the Greeks,
I'd see all the fighting
And mathematical geeks.

I'd go and meet Hitler
When he was a child
Try to make him care
And become more mild.

At the end of my journey
I'd come back to today
History is in the past
And it'll stay that way!

Bethany Apedaile (14)
Lomond School

FLIGHT SOUTH FOR THE WINTER

We started as ten from Scotland,
The number growing higher as we flew south across Europe.
What beautiful countryside we passed,
Not going too fast so we could be left with pictures in our heads,
That we could describe to our kids when they're tucked up in their beds.

With the change of air currents there was no need to stop for rests
But every now and then we did to take a breath,
And take in the views.
Small villages, French vineyards,
Rivers and mountains,
Italian farm houses with their olive groves.

But when we were higher in the sky
There were other views.
Clouds of different shapes and sizes
Beautiful sunsets with attractive pinks, yellows and oranges,
Rainbows reaching far to the horizon.

What a shock our flock had
When we heard bullets being fired into the sky.
We decided to fly even higher
And soon the bullets were out of range.

When we reached our destination,
We had a great celebration.
We were in warmth and safety now in Africa
But the celebrations did not last all the night
As we were too tired after our long flight.

Alicia Barham (13)
Lomond School

THE SNAKE

Maddening, marble-like, malicious eyes,
Casually turned and the snake gave a meaningless sigh,
Its smooth scales reflecting the calm, moonlit sky.

Uncertainty spread through the creature's path
As, suddenly, startling shadows passed
And its silencing hiss resembled a cold, cruel laugh.

It slid in an elegant rhythm of such grace,
Slithering at a gentle, enchanting pace,
Silent and speedy yet with no true haste.

Fearless, fugitive with features of pride,
In complete control and just starting to glide,
Surely a snake with nothing to hide . . .?

Fangs like daggers, a poisonous bite,
A razor-sharp tongue and eyes alight,
But most importantly, the solid courage inside.

With a clever use of its effective sixth sense,
The sly snake did pause but then slowly recommenced,
Adrenaline rising, muscles tense.

Nowhere was safe yet danger was rare,
The surreptitious snake slid on without a care,
Solemn, silent, beautiful, bare . . .

Kirsty Baynham (13)
Lomond School

IMPRISONMENT

When it's summer term at school
When children shout, laugh and play,
And I am stuck at home in bed with flu,
In horrible, lonely, darkness,
There must be better ways
To spend my days.

I lie in my bed,
Looking up at the ceiling,
Just letting my thoughts go by
There is no time in my room
I just leave it go on by.

The school lunch bell wakes me
In the silence of my room
It echoes in my ears
I hear the children playing, laughing and having fun
I feel very alone.

Mum said I must keep my curtains shut,
Or else I'll get no sleep
So my room is dark, except for a few gaps
Where the sunshine creeps in,
And reminds me of playing outside
Everything in my room starts to have a hazy outline
And I fall asleep.

I am woken by my brother's laughter
As he starts to run upstairs,
I have my dinner then back to sleep
When I wake in the morning Mum reminds me
I have another long day ahead of me
My room feels like a prison cell.

Rachael Cameron (11)
Lomond School

WE TRAVELLED

It was winter,
The snow lay thickly on the ground,
Icicles hung from every tree,
And we travelled.

We knew not where we were going
Or whether it would be better,
Better than what we had left,
But still, we travelled.

For ten long years we have lived,
Lived in the hell of imprisonment.
Now, we were free, like birds,
And we travelled.

We walked, through countryside and towns,
Towns where we bought food,
With the little money we had
And we travelled.

Soon it was spring,
The snow long gone,
And the grass as green as could be,
Yet still, we travelled.

We came to a village,
A small, sweet village,
The people so full of kindness,
That we travelled no longer.

Fiona Milton (12)
Lomond School

IMPRISONMENT

All you could see was grey,
And all you could feel was the dampness,
All alone in the
Dark, bare room.

You got used to little food,
But the smell made you hungry,
You didn't get much to drink,
So your mouth got very dry.

You didn't allow yourself to think
Because thinking would make you smart,
You didn't try to escape,
Because you knew the consequences.

You made very little friends,
And you spoke to almost no one,
You told no one your name,
Unless it was necessary.

Abbie Williamson (11)
Lomond School

MY JOURNEY THROUGH THE STARS

My journey
Flying round the stars,
Floating past the planets,
Soaring through the solar system.

My journey
Colours whizzing past,
Spinning by so fast,
Twirling round the universe.

My journey,
Dancing back to Earth,
My feet touch the ground,
My magical journey ends.

Laura Carver (13)
Lomond School

IN THE FUTURE

What shall I be?
Sailing the seven seas
Or a motor car driver?
No, a doctor
What on Earth will I be?

I think I'll be a rugby player!
No, no I can't decide,
It's killing me what will I be?
How about a funny clown
Or what about a scientist?

Will I be a member of a band
Or a programmer?
I'm thinking, I'm thinking what will I be?
A teacher, no, I wouldn't stand the children
Will I be a simple coffee boy?

What will I decide to be?
A businessman travelling the world,
I could be a poet,
Or a zoo keeper.
I know I'll be a TV presenter.

Euan Millar (11)
Lomond School

IMPRISONMENT

All around is barbed wire,
With sentries patrolling everywhere.
We have nowhere to go and
Nothing to look forward to,
The days run into each other,
And time seems to stand still.

Sometimes I dream of home,
And I have to pinch myself,
When I wake up.

Will I ever get out of here?
Will I be able to see my family again?
If we give up hope then all is lost.
We must keep on going.

Kirsty Cameron (11)
Lomond School

THE NIGHT

I remember all the cold nights,
I would lie waiting in the dark.
Pitch-black
I would lie there every night,
In the cold.

Hours would pass and I still could not sleep,
I could hear other boys screaming for 'home' a place I knew little of.
Home, it was a place I knew only as a small, grey room,
I had been here since I was four
The words, 'mother', 'father' and 'family' meant nothing to me.

In the middle of the night I heard noises,
Birds in the trees,
The wind blowing through trees,
And occasionally rain.
These sounds became familiar to me,
They were my friends.

When daylight came I cried,
Thinking about the torture I was to go through and I prayed,
For the night, the pitch-black and . . .
My friends, the noises.

Jenna MacLeod (12)
Lomond School

BIRDS

Flying, diving,
Ready to go,
Ready to flee
The winter snow.

Carolling, whistling,
Beginning to sing,
Looking forward
To everything.

Diving, swooping,
Arriving back,
Ready to nest,
Raise a young family.

Gathering, teaching,
The work never ends
Until the family
Split for all time.

Heather Barnes (15)
Madras College

LOOK

A million stories shine brightly
In this dark, starry sky
A million voices laugh, sing and sigh.

High up above the world
In the deep, velvet sky
They hide thousands of stories
Hidden by the bright, night stars.

If you are sad,
If you are lonely,
All to do is
Look.
Look and imagine
Forget the rest of the world
There is only you
You alone with thousands of waiting stories.

Trust what I write to you
You may not see them at first
Look harder
For there is a story in every star
There is a story for everyone
Let your imagination run
And discover
That they are truly there.

They are calling to you
Answer them,
Discover them,
Reach beyond the heights of the stars and discover them.

Charis Bredin (12)
Madras College

THE SOLAR SYSTEM

Planets going around the sun
Nine in all, total sum
One is boiled, the next even worse
And the planet in third is planet Earth.

Next-door neighbour, number four
Planet of red, the unknown and war,
World of unknown mystery,
Is there something that hasn't been seen?

King of the worlds, biggest by far,
Is the giant planet of Jupiter,
Oranges and reds, ambers and yellows galore,
The giant red spot, the thousands year storm.

Saturn a world of illustrious fame,
But for its rings, not just the name,
Rings of ice, rock, dust and satellites,
Orbiting Saturn in its glorious might.

Next along, the world of ice,
Of Uranus and Neptune,
Distant from earthling eyes,
Millions of miles past far flung moons.

Orbits the planet number nine,
Smallest of the planets
Icy rock of frozen time,
And of the day and dark and barely lit.

Past the planet we do not know
What lies out there in space,
Whatever it is will be long wondered so,
By the human race.

Jack Shepherd (13)
Madras College

EMOTIONALLY BRUISED

I have been hurt once again
The cruel, cold-hearted words, which slice,
Right through the silence of awkwardness.
This is the worst emotion, to fall in love and get
Your heart torn apart at such a young age.
They try to comfort me but not one of them
Actually know how I'm feeling.
Why can't they see that nothing will be the same?
I will never be the same as when I was.
He has taken a part of me that I can't regain
For his evil mind.
Why does it hurt inside so much?
The burning red inside of me is
Devouring my insides.
I keep asking myself how someone could
Just taking another one's life and act as if
It's theirs to keep
I feel alone
No one to talk to, no one to care
My mind and soul is shattered by one person
I will never forgive them
I can't forgive them.

Marcie Sturrock (15)
Madras College

THE AMERICAN TRAGEDY

My departure from school, just one of many,
Chatting with friends some dull, some funny.

Unaware of tragic events, from earlier in the day,
I arrived home to find, shock and dismay.

Disbelieves and sympathy filled my head,
For families and friends of those who are dead.

Terrorists are so cold-hearted and selfish,
Taking the lives of the innocent and helpless.

I think and dwell on the hurt and the pain,
I hope the world will never suffer again.

There's nothing I can do and nothing I can say,
To make the grief and hurt go away.

Tonight I know, I'll lie awake in bed
Attempting to accept what may lie ahead.

Sara Gray (15)
Maxwelltown High School

NED THE PUNK PIG

Ned the punk pig,
He was so bad
Ned the punk pig,
He killed his own dad.

Ned the punk pig,
He was always in trouble
One day he was caught,
That burst his bubble.

Ned the punk pig,
He was sent to jail
One day he escaped, he shouted
'I knew evil would prevail!'

He fled and fled for months
Until he was caught, the sinner
Even though he protested
He ended up as Christmas dinner.

Annabell Kelly (12)
Millburn Academy

DRAGON ISLAND

On the boat the four did stand
And spied the country from the sea
King Edmund and King Caspian
Eustance and Queen Lucy.

They anchored in a shallow bay
And set out to search the land
Through high and low they searched and found
A castle, big and grand.

Around the castle they did go
But no door or drawbridge found
Only a notice on the wall
With ivy growing round.

They gathered round, King Caspian read
'For all of you who seek
The magic key to enter here
In the dragon's lair doth sleep!'

So out across the land they went
To find the dragon's home.
Near and far until they spied
A cave carved in the stone.

Out from the darkness a bellow blew
And out the dragon came.
It howled up Lucy out of reached
The others fled the flame.

Far from the hill the others stopped
They sat down on the ground.
They tired and tried to hatch a plan
And sat 'til one was found.

Back to the cave the trio ran
Then Caspian moved aside
The rest then called the dragon out
A flame came from inside.

Soon they found that Lucy lived
And Edmund ran to save her
All the while King Caspian's spear
Flew straight without a waver.

Caspian's spear had killed the beast
While Eustance in he ran
Straight for the cave to get the key
And came back out, good man!

The gates to the castle were open
To the joy of everyone.
And here they stayed for ever more
At last their work was done.

Jean Bain (12)
Millburn Academy

MISS JONES

Miss Marie Jones, spinster of the parish
Loved and lived for her sweetheart John
But she wasted her life in pursuit of marriage
The chance of which had come and gone.

> John, a tall, dark swarthy gent
> Worked hard to keep his reputation high
> His wife although, she did not know
> Another woman would make her cry.

Secret meetings came and went
Amid the bustle of daily life
Harder and harder it came to be
To keep his secret from his wife.

> The wife of John one day found out
> Her husband's darkest lies
> She made it her business to avenge
> And plotted her rival's demise.

One cold and dark November night
Slipped out of the house undercover
Her plan she practised time and time again
To murder her husband's lover.

> She tapped so gently on the door
> And waited for a reply
> Plunged a dagger deep into Marie's heart
> And vowed that she must die.

Poor Marie Jones she staggered back
Blood pouring from her chest
She cried out for John, her only love
As she laid herself to rest.

John never knew it was his wife
Who cruelly murdered his mistress
He spent the rest of his days
So sad and full of distress.

This tale is as sad as it would seem
One full of woe and regret
About a love that could never be
And the death that Marie met.

Carlie Borthwick (13)
Millburn Academy

MY BALLAD

There was a girl called Mary
She was incredibly pretty
The boy she liked was handsome Mike
He was so tall and witty.

It was upon their wedding night
When they exchanged the rings
They were hoping for such happiness
In all that the future brings.

A family quickly followed
After their first year together
They worked hard to provide needs
In all kinds of weather.

Calamity then came their way
Mike took ill and soon was dead
With not a moment to spare
They put him in a coffin lined with lead.

Kerrie Goddard (12)
Millburn Academy

THE BALLAD OF ARROWSORN AND VENIXCROSS

A duchess once bore
Two babies fair
To become wizards was their destiny
But now they were cuddly with no hair.

The duke decided to split the two
They screamed and yelled,
They kicked and shouted, if only he knew
Now they were blue in the face and their nappies smelled.

They grew as time passed
Fair Arrowsorn of white
With gleaming eyes and shining white hair
Decided for certain it was good, he'd fight.

Some miles away
Cruel Venixcross decided to slay
With dark hair and coal-black eyes
For evil he would fight as he may.

So then they were men
Each more than six feet tall
Broad, rich, proud and very wise
Living in no grandeur castle or hall.

Off they went to Sunrise Vale
They carried evil, they carried good
They travelled in day and travelled in night
Good and evil met as each knew it would.

They were full of fear
'Who are you?' Arrowsorn cried
Venixcross thought very hard then said:
'I'm Grievendiel of evil' he stupidly lied.

They bowed and began to duel
They fought with all their might
With clever wands and bright staffs
I've never seen such a gruesome sight!

They stopped, stared
'Brother Venixcross' Arrowsorn sighed
'I'm sorry brother' Venixcross said sadly
Arrowsorn turned round, Venixcross died.

Stumbly and cursing
He turns and walks slowly home
Arrowsorn cried, yelled and shouted
How he wishes he'd just known.

Eilidh Gunn (12)
Millburn Academy

STAN AND THE TELEPHONE MAN

One early morning in June
An arrogant young man called Stan
Rented an office, a desk and a phone
Stan the man had a master plan.

Into his office a fat man appeared
Important Stan pretended to phone
He talked of negotiating an important deal
As he tried to impress, his confidence was shown.

As he ended the call, success on his face
'Can I help you?' said in a most proper tone
'But no' said the workman, a smile on his lips
'If I may help you by connecting your phone.'

Neil Holmes (11)
Millburn Academy

THE PRICE OF FAME

Cynthia Sally Smith dreamed of being famous,
Dressing all rich and posh
She went to a singing competition
To win a lot of dosh.

The queue was long and noisy
She stood there in the cold,
Dripping wet and feeling small,
She didn't feel too bold.

When finally she got inside,
And took a front row seat,
The people stood and stared,
What had she on her feet?

Down she looked and there she saw,
Pink and fluffy, black and white
On the left her brother's soccer slipper,
And her bunny on the right!

'Up on the stage,' the compere called
Cynthia had to go
She kicked her slippers to the side
Time to put on a show!

Like a Hollywood star she made her way
Bare foot and with a smile
She glided smoothly through the crowd
Boy, did she have style!

Cameras flashed and clicked and whirled
When up the stairs she rose
But little knowing, there it hung,
A bogey up her nose.

Cynthia Sally Smith is famous now
She's going to appear on Parky
But she'd rather it was because she sang
Not for needing a hanky!

Hannah McLaren (12)
Millburn Academy

TOM AND LISA

Tom and Lisa went to the pub
Then they went through the door
The pub was busy all around
Lots of people on the dance floor.

Lisa sat down in a corner
While Tom got the drinks
Lisa was looking around scared
Tom noticed and gave her some winks.

'I'm not happy here' Lisa said,
'I don't mind going too.'
'Alright' said Tom and took his coat
'Hang on, I'm not finished with you!'

The man who said this looked fierce
He pulled a shiny silver gun out of his sleeve
Tom and him started fighting
Lisa her eyes couldn't believe.

A doctor came out of the pub
And saw bodies covered in mud
Lisa crying in the middle
Her face was spread of blood.

James Cameron (13)
Millburn Academy

THE DISAPPOINTED BRIDE

The family sat and ate their meal,
 Looking at the clock,
They talked and laughed and ate their food,
 And then there came a knock.

They opened up the big, brown door,
 And there they saw a man,
He looked so handsome and so nice,
 He came in a large, black van.

The pretty girl in a long, red dress
 Could not believe her eyes,
She fell in love with one big glance
 'You are my man!' she cried.

'I've come to check your gas, my dear,
 I think you've got a leak,
I'll try and fix it with my tools,
 I'll come and see next week!'

They fell in love and kissed on the cheek,
 He asked her for her hand,
They married then in a lovely church,
 She wore a golden band.

They went to live in Africa,
 But when they got the post,
He turned all white and disappeared . . .
 He really was a ghost!

Claire Bates (11)
Millburn Academy

THE BATTLE FOR THE THRONE

When dawn came in the break of light
As the sun came out
The war cries sound
As they scream and shout.

The king and a prince fought over the throne
The king said 'I will have you dead'
The prince wanted revenge,
He said, 'I will have your head!'

The swish of an arrow cut the air
The prince's leg was pierced, he was crying
People endlessly dropping around him
And there was a sad sense of dying.

The king lay still and breathless
A hard last battle he endured
While his opponent prince across the way
Lay bloodied but alive, only injured.

His motion was noticed by the king's soldiers
They made sure he was killed
The prince's pain now over,
His grave shall now be filled.

With no victors
The battle had been lost
Blood-stained, the battlefield
How many lives it had cost.

The queen in her honour
Her son as successor she chose
The new prince was celebrated
His supporters cheered him from their rows.

Gordon Wilson (12)
Millburn Academy

THE KILLER

There was a boy called Shorty
Who went to a school disco
And he got bullied
By a boy called Jon Brisco.

They next day Shorty moved house
He was my good friend
But he had to leave
He said our friendship had to end.

Thirty years later in an alley
Brisco was found bloody and dead
When he was found
He had no head.

We decided to go to Shorty's old house
It was dark and very scary
And up on the main wall
Was a picture of Queen Mary.

In the house we found some food
And in the kitchen there was a knife
And in the bath in a mess
Was Brisco's horrible wife.

At night we went out
To try and catch the horrible man
When we were out of hope
Round the corner came a big, white van.

When he stepped out of the van
He shouted 'I'll add you to my tally'
We were so scared
We belted it down the alley.

When he ran after us
He said, 'You won't get away'
But when he turned the corner
He fell over a bundle of hay.

When he pulled off his mask
And Shorty we saw
Out of his jacket
Fell a rusty old saw.

When he was found guilty
He said 'That is wrong'
The judge yelled get him out of here
So Shorty sang a song.

Ten years later I was happy
Until I got some mail
I opened it and realised
That it was from the jail.

It said 'Run away'
I wondered what for
And when it said Shorty had escaped
I got my shotgun out of the drawer.

When I heard a knock
I opened the door
And when I saw Shorty
I shot him to the floor.

When I had noticed
What I had done
I finally decided
To have some fun.

Christopher Raffan (12)
Millburn Academy

FATAL FOREST

There is a wood
Near to my home
It's dark and creepy
And overgrown.

People don't go there
Because they're afraid
Of things that might
Come out of the shade.

It is said
That the woods are cursed
Anybody who goes there
Ends up for the worst.

A house beside the wood
Was recently sold
The family who bought it
Were definitely bold.

In moved the Wilsons
Early one day
With their two children
Danny and Kay.

The children decided
One sunny day
Into the woods
They would go to play.

Deep in the woods
They walked around
Then Kay saw footprints
On the ground.

Danny felt brave
'Let's follow them now.'
But Kay wasn't sure
'If we get lost we'll get a row.'

Danny set off
So Kay decided to follow
They soon found themselves
In a hollow.

The footprints ended
At the bottom of a tree
And Danny said
'Who could it be?'

Then suddenly a creature
Hung down from the tree
And lifted up Danny
Like he was a flea.

Kay ran and ran
Without looking back
But she got lost
And couldn't find the track.

When lunch was ready
Their mother went out
'Come in for lunch.'
She cried with a shout.

When they weren't there
She started to worry
Then called the police
In a big hurry.

When the police came round
They went into the wood
They searched and searched
As much as they could.

In the middle of the wood
They found an old church
And beside it was Danny
Hanging from a birch.

Their mother screamed
And turned around
Only to find Kay
Lying dead on the ground.

After the events which
Happened that day
Mr and Mrs Wilson
Moved far away.

Andrew Moffat (11)
Millburn Academy

THE MAKINLEW MERMAIDS

As the dawn of the day broke
Over the town of Barnhabrew
A man was leaving his family
To sail the ocean blue.

This man, he was John Makinlew
And mighty gullible was he
'You'll catch the plague if you stay any longer,
My friend,' said his worst enemy!

So now poor John was sailing the sea
And not enjoying it one bit
He was seasick, fevered and not well fed
And his room was by moonlight lit.

Upon this night a storm did rise
The wind howled like never before
The ship was tossed like a cork
'Til Johnny's poor head was sore.

Then suddenly above, a wave did rise
This wave was taller than towers
It then crashed down on the pitiful ship
With all of its awesome powers!

The ship broke in two like a matchstick
And sank to the bottom of the blue
There were no survivors of that we are sure
Except one: Mr J Makinlew!

So Johnny did swim for two days and a night
Until he could swim no more
But just as Johnny was going to give up
His feet hit a watery shore!

After a week on this island
Johnny of this was sure
'I am alone, by myself,' he said
'Not even a fish can I lure!'

Until one day Johnny sat on a rock
Wondering what to do
When there in a pool beside the sea
He spied five mermaids blue.

Desperate was he to find a companion
And they looked beautiful and smart
He ran and swam straight over to them
'Tis bad that they'd steal his heart.

They took him back to their world
Under the sea was it
Castles, towns, halls and thrones
By sunlight were they lit.

The man was fed a feast of fish
And entertained by many
But he longed for his own sweet house
Family and dogs, Bic and Benny.

Finally, the mermaids had had enough
Of his moaning, groaning and cries
So they took him prisoner in a castle cell
And rejoiced at the reduction of noise.

So John spent two days in this cell
Crying all the while
'Oh wife, oh children, oh dogs far away
I'll come back to thee with a smile.'

The mermaids thought
Oh what have we done?
It wasn't our fault . . .
We thought you had fun!

So the mermaids tried again to be nice
But it didn't turn out very well
Johnny said, 'I'm going to stay put
And die in this awful cell.

And die shall I, bon voyage, au revoir
I'll stay no longer down here.'
Then he left the Earth, he was no more
With a great big sob and a tear!

Then the mermaids felt as bad as could be
For what they had done to 'you know who'
And vowed never again to go near us
In memory of John Makinlew (RIP).

And that is why, you simply will not see
A mermaid in your life
Or if you do, remember poor Johnny
Who left his kids and wife!

Anna MacLeod (12)
Millburn Academy

FATAL MEDICINE

In a doctor's surgery
Which was nice and kind
An evil doctor, Frank got hired
The owner must have been blind.

Frank had come from far away
He had come with bad intentions
He wanted to kill the people
With things I would not like to mention.

The next day
The first patient came in
'What is wrong?'
Said Frank with a grin.

'I have a sore back
It's giving me pain'
Frank said 'Take this pill
And you'll be fine again.'

Frank laughed loudly
As the man fell to the floor
Then he chucked the body
Out the back door.

Frank then killed many more
With his lethal pills
He got stronger and stronger
With each person he killed.

One day some policemen came over
And looked in horror at what they found
Hundreds of dead bodies
Lying on the ground.

The police searched for the evil doctor
They searched for many a day
They couldn't find Frank anywhere
What could they say.

In a wood quite near
There the doctor lay
He became weaker and weaker
He wouldn't live another day.

Frank had become sick and tired
He had become too strong
He knew this would happen
He'd lived far too long.

The police found his dead body
Lying there in the wood
They didn't know how this event happened
But they knew it was very good.

Eilidh Moffat (11)
Millburn Academy

THE WORST WOOD

Deep, dark and treacherous
Is the wood of Hellish Grove
With trees as high as skyscrapers
And blood-stained leaves of mauve.

In the gruesome forest
There lives an evil witch
With evil eyes and crooked nose
Her name is Eliza Glitch.

This bad witch has evil powers
She works with the forces of darkness
She uses them for all the wrong reasons
Eliza Glitch is heartless.

One day in the terrible Hellish Grove
Two walkers with some heavy packs
Sat beneath the tall chestnut tree
And ate their tasty snacks.

Eliza in her evil ways had to get rid of them
Her eerie voice echoed through the woods
'I'll catch you if I can!
You will be *my* delicious food!'

'Who are you and where are you?'
Shouted one petrified walker
Then a reply 'You'd better watch out
For I am an evil stalker!'

Out of a chestnut tree came Eliza
With a long, sharp carving knife
A bag with no breathing holes
Will she take a life?

'I've got you now, you ugly walkers
Now you are going to die.'
I won't go into too much detail
I'd really rather not try.

We're not sure how and don't know when
But Eliza disappeared
She must have vanished into thin air
How very uncanny and weird.

I hope Eliza never comes back
I know the walkers are dead
The Hellish Grove still stands
But nobody there does tread.

Kirsty Hogg (12)
Millburn Academy

THE THREE FRIENDS

The three friends met one day
They took their boat and headed out to sea,
To catch some fish was their aim
To take them home for tea.

It was all going well for the boys
Suddenly it went all wrong
There was a storm heading their way
They were frightened so they all sang a song.

They all started to panic
Because the boat was heading for a rock
They all started to run around
They stopped when they heard a big knock.

'Quick! Into the life raft we must go
Out boat is going - call mayday!'
The boys all rushed to the side
'We're all done for' they say.

Here came a safety helicopter
They shouted happily we're safe, hooray,
Up the helicopter ladder we all shall go
We are all alive! No way!

Ian Craigie (11)
Millburn Academy

THAT'S WHAT BUDDIES ARE FOR

There was Jimmy from Croy and Willie from Nairn
One was aye happy, the other a girn
They fell out one day about what to play
Was it footie or fishing they just couldn't say.

They argued a while, both with frowns, not a smile
They parted and went their own ways
Willie went to the burn with his rod and his worms
When he slipped, banged his head and was dazed.

Jimmy from the football ground saw poor Willie falling down
He dropped his ball and ran over cos Willie's head was underwater
He dragged poor Willie by the feet
Out of the burn and over a seat.

His back he gave a heafty whack
Till Willie's breathing did come back
He coughed and spluttered for a while
Then he saw his best friend's smile.

Willie'd never been so grateful
To have his friend so close, so faithful
For Willie's frown came off that day
And a smile of friendship was to stay.

Cara Cruickshank (12)
Millburn Academy

THE BALLAD OF WRESTLING

The hall was packed the lights were bright
The crowd let out a cheer
The bell rang, the wrestlers fought
The wrestlers showed no fear.

The Rock shouted, 'Kane, I'm going to win!
You do not stand a chance!'
But Kane said 'You are going to lose!
I'll make you hop and dance!'

Then Kane sprang up and hit The Rock
He bounced on to the rope
And fell back into a head lock
Which made him cough.

Kane was about to do a chokeslam
When Rock moved to one side
Kane moved forward to grab him
But fell over the ropes and died.

The moral of this ballad
Shows that wrestling is not fake
The wrestlers must be brave and fit
It is for their own sake.

Andrew Reid (12)
Millburn Academy

A REMOTE CONTROL

Am I not free?
Unborn by responsibility,
My mind clean, powerful; a tool
On which the cosmos can be carved?
And yet, within:
Faded reruns, shadows of oft seen spectacles;
An endless loop; a needle skipping the groove, in vein:
A blip on memory.

And, the braying hoards whining,
Whooping.
And sighing? Whispering?
But the three billion muses
Commenting on the cycle:
'Now you must laugh - yes! Now!
And now . . . weep - *oh weep you!*'

The machine killing.

The mind - I want to imagine again;
To be seven years again.
Nonsense talk! March hares! Explaining trees
By lost old me I could touch
And learn.

Stephen O'Toole (16)
St Columba's High School, Gourock

THE FIRST JOURNEY OF THE DAY

My school bag hangs heavy
On my shoulder
Footsteps falling short
Of my usual stride,
Plodding up to school
For morning prayers.

The wind is channelled through the Pends
Causing me to shiver silently
I hug my coat more tightly,
Onward I walk with my mute companions.

School buildings loom nearer
A cluster of girls dressed in green
The janitor opens the door and nods
I feel my head return the gesture
As I climb the stairs.

I fall with a sigh
Into one of the ordered chairs
Close my eyes, thinking back to my bed
My trance is broken
The clang from the organ heralds the start of another day.

Abigail Elphinstone (17)
St Leonards School, St Andrews

THE GRANDFATHER CLOCK

Now shabby and decrepit,
It stands in the corner,
Collecting dust,
Its legs wobbly with age,
Despite its elderliness
It has the story to tell
Of its journey
Since the time of its construction.

Since that time it has stood in many halls,
Visited several places,
Stared face to face with countless people,
Seen things that nobody else has.
It does not just tell you the present time,
But about the past too.
It has been on a journey
Which we will never be able to learn about.

Fiona Hendrie (14)
St Leonards School, St Andrews

TRAPPED

The arrows flash with acid red
The metal meets in the middle
I am trapped
Swallowed by a box of steel.

Inside my stomach,
Horses are galloping up hills,
Hearts beating, hair wispy in the wind
As the box is hauled towards the heavens.

The box is closing in on me,
The walls are getting nearer,
Or are they?
I can't breathe.

Suddenly
The horses reach the top of their hill
All is still
And the box is halted.

The metal divides once again,
And the third floor meets the eye.

Margaret Houston (12)
St Leonards School, St Andrews

RACING FOR TIME

On your marks, get set, go
My heart's beating
Like a big bass drum
The fifteen hundred is way too long.
I kept telling my games captain,
I can't do this and never will.

I look up and everyone is a little dot,
All I hear is my breathing,
It sounds so different.

Here's everyone coming,
But they are on their last lap
Racy Rachel is coming first,
And silly Sally is coming second.

I don't mind being last
At least it gives everyone else the chance.

Frances Lindesay-Bethune (15)
St Leonards School, St Andrews

DESTINATION

Here I lay,
Still and breathless,
Just like always,
Who cares what's behind?

Roll these windows down
This cool night is curious
Let the world look in
Who cares who sees anything?

Take me around again,
Get me out of this place,
I want to break free,
The past is meaningless.

Drive faster,
Take me anywhere
I am still your passenger
I have no destination.

Callum Steven (18)
St Leonards School, St Andrews

THE LIFE OF AN HOUR

Tick-tock!
Look at the clock
A new lifespan
Of an hour has began.

Each hand of the clock
Has its own move.
Not every hour goes
By the same groove.

Time never waits
Nor takes a break,
Even if we're not ready
Life's beat is steady.

Once an hour's ended,
It can't be lived again
When we finish our run
That's that life done.

Farjana Chowdhury (14)
St Leonards School, St Andrews

A DOVE FLIES OUT

The animals plod on to the ark,
Floorboards creak
A light patter of rain bounces on the grass
Giraffes stretch their necks to nibble tender leaves.

A door locks, clicking shut
A golden bolt parts the sky
Rumbling thunder grumbles
Rain drops, dripping on noses, dripping, dropping.

Water starts to rise to screams
Gurgling, squelching, making many bubbles
The world below is engulfed by the ravenous sea
But this is only the start
Of a journey on the oceans.

For now the ark is afloat,
Alive with songs and sounds,
For forty days, floating,
Forty nights floating and dripping.

A dove flies out, returns
The journey's end is near.

Annabel Reid (11)
St Leonards School, St Andrews

JOURNEYS

The engine started and hearse pulled away
It had power over the roads, cars stopped to stare
And trails of mourning family members followed
As though they were on their way to doom.

The long, black, stretched car leads the way
Inside the vehicle there was silence
Peaceful yet disturbing, flowers signalled
The love that others felt for the deceased.

Yet no one knows where her spirit is now
Or if her journey through time is over
The drive lasted for eternity
More so by the eerie, sharp silence.

The peace was dedicated to the young girl
Her life had been cut short, she was cheated
From the chance of happiness and freedom
Now she was captured, no one can help her.

Sarah Watson (16)
St Leonards School, St Andrews

THE PASSING

As she looks out of the window
It becomes a gateway to a world.
Inside the rustic smell becomes a friend
To which will be her last.
Her body grows old now and her only escape is sleep.
The furniture dents the once old carpet
Now a blur of orange and brown
She stares out of the window entranced
By sailing leaves and the hypnotising pattern of feet.
Her legs become stiff now and every movement is a challenge.
Now she is drifting away from her once permanent world
Drifting through time, darkness and life
She sees faces, colours and places to which she will never return.
She hears voices, which are a sweet reminder of her past
Her vision is clear now and she is sailing past
Her once meaningful life towards a barrier.
It's over, she now rests in a dark room
To which will become her new and last friend.

Jennifer Watson (14)
St Leonards School, St Andrews

CHAOS

Doors swing
We descend to the cool breeze
A drone.

Girls chat and sing
Escape the chaos
Walk, run, trip, fall,
Lie still.

Obscure images, thoughts and past conversations
Whiz around in our heads
Confusion.

Walk, run, dance, faster and faster
Stop.

Turn and talk
Rain beats on our heads
Sheer delight.
Movement and singing
Water runs along the road.

The doors swing
We descend to the dry warmth
Music, television, food, food and more
Exhaustion
Muddled heads.

The supernatural and reality merge
Happily unaware of the meaning
All is forgotten with daybreak.

Harriet Patterson (16)
St Leonards School, St Andrews

THE YEAR

The fresh dew sparkles
Shining icicles drop from the telegraph poles,
As the morning sun peeps from beneath its blanket
Not yet ready to awake.

The garden is plentiful
Branches bend under the weight of laden trees.
Young thrush pluck sweetened plums
Off the topmost branches.

Golden brown leaves swirl at my feet
I trudge through the multicoloured mounds beneath.
I quicken my pace,
Thoughts of holidays springing to my mind.

Thick snow falls,
Gently flowing down,
Concealing bulbs that are preparing for spring.
Animals sleep in their hidden dens
After the good harvest
They fear no danger.

A year ends
I look back and see change.
Until spring dawns again
I wait, for the daffodils to nod,
And for the birds' sweet song.

Winter is here,
But the world turns forever.

Eilidh Reid (13)
St Leonards School, St Andrews

INSOMNIAC

As you turn your head from side to side
Colourful patterns appear on the walls;
Circles, squares and triangles.
Weird snowflake shapes and long curvy splodges.
Red, green, yellow, blue, purple, orange,
Silver and gold sparkles.
The patterns move like a sea of waves
Swishing and swirling they go.
The turquoise calm is overcome with the deep blue and the near black.
The patterns submerge then spread then re-merge.
A noise, rustling and humming and footsteps
Louder and closer then away.
There is a potent smell, a smell of delight and calm.
There is considerable familiarity in the darkness
The senses are heightened
As tiredness sets in, the mind races
Round and round go thought and image.
Faster and faster yet concentration is absent.
Sheer exhaustion overcomes the body and mind
At last pure, nothing is obtained.
The mind can finally rest as the eyes close
Softly, slowly, gently.
The murmur of the wind outside is soothing
There is a distant moan of cars on the road.
And then
Sleep.

Eleanor Cooke (15)
St Leonards School, St Andrews

DUKE OF EDINBURGH - BACKPACK ON! BACKPACK OFF!

As we waken,
Reality strikes;
Mixed emotions hit us.

Out of the tent
Frost-bitten.
Grim prospects ahead.

Attacked by midges,
As we bravely battle
To the bothy.

Backpack on!

Facing vertical hills
Treacherous weather
We trek, we trek and we trek!

Sweaty and suffering, we struggle
In search of the summit,
Where sun and sustenance greet us.

Backpack off!

Biscuit after biscuit
Nibble after nibble
We rest.

Blistered feet,
Bitten - up and down
Aching limbs
'It's over, it's done!'
A sigh of relief from everyone.

Backpack off!

Amy McPhail (14)
St Leonards School, St Andrews

A JOURNEY

It swooped and landed
On the tip of an ancient colonnade,
The sun setting fire
To every feather.
In its beak
An olive branch,
Fruitful;
Jewels glistening,
Deep purple.
Plucked from a grove
Hidden well, a secret,
Many miles from here
A precious gift carried swiftly.

This journey, so perilous
The fearless firebird undertook.
Great stretches of golden sand
Among the camels;
Tree to tree
With the monkeys;
Overcrowded streets
Above fire-eaters, jugglers;
Gliding through the mists
At the summits of mountains.

The destination now reached
On an island uncharted,
The bird opened its beak -
The burden dropped,
Onto the earth,
An olive tree
Will grow.

Catherine Hood (14)
St Leonards School, St Andrews

SEA TRIP

The sky is blue,
The sea is green,
My bag is ruby-red.
The boat is white,
The dock is tan,
My hat is on my head.

The gulls cry,
The captain calls,
A dog barks to him.
The wind whistles,
The waves splash,
A little boy takes a swim.

The boat rocks,
The waves swell,
Our sails billow in the wind.
The water splashes,
The sun feels warm
Our trip is near its end.

The sea is salty,
The air is fresh,
I love this kind of day,
The coastline nears
The fish smell strong
I can see Tampa Bay.

Carolyn Nielsen (12)
St Leonards School, St Andrews

JOURNEYS

I'm travelling alone,
I don't know where to,
Or for how long,
All I know is,
I want to be with you.

The meadows are yellow,
The pastures are green,
I watch the world
Pass by my windscreen,
And all I can think of is you.

The sun warms my face,
The wind wakens me,
I'm still sitting here,
For your face to appear.

The train pulls in,
The engine stops,
I pick up my case,
And get off the train,
As always you are there,
Standing in the rain.

I leap into your clutch,
Your warmth surrounds me,
The world disappears,
My journey is over.

Rosie Sugden (13)
St Leonards School, St Andrews

IN AFRICA

There are people everywhere
To look at and stare.
Women, men
There were lots of them.

I walked along dusty roads,
With passing truck loads
Of children laughing, crying,
Some close to dying.

Stalls of many magnificent things,
Women selling their belongings,
To pay for food, to give their family
To help them live their lives happily.

Going on safari, is the best of all,
Listening to the birds' call,
Giraffes, elephants, lots to see,
All kinds of wasps and bees.

Africa, a wonderful place
People of every human race
Where ever you go,
People to know.

Babies dying,
Mothers crying.
The journey that this has been,
Is more than anyone can dream.

Katharine Cooke (14)
St Leonards School, St Andrews

JOURNEY TO THE CHEESE

There it was
Upon the shelf
That golden treasure
All for himself
That wonderful trophy
Sat on a plate
He needed to get it
Before it's too late.

Silently creeping
He scampered near.
Keeping alert
For what he could hear.
He climbed up the table
And spotted his goal
Grabbed it with pleasure
And ran for his hole.

Then she came
Out of the blue
He suddenly realised
What he had to do
He ran as she chased him
He took a great dive.
Slid into his hole
Proud of his prize.

As he sat,
On the hard floor
Eating away
Near to the door
He thought of the journey
That he'd have to make.
The very next morning
To take back the plate!

Kerry Grainger (12)
St Leonards School, St Andrews

JOURNEY TO A PARADISE

The noise of the wind
Whispers at my ear
Waves lap
On the calm shores.

A gentle sea salt breeze
Is in the air
The sea
Conducts its orchestra.

The luxury island
Draws ever closer
Palm trees
Reflected in the crystal water.

The arrival is hailed
By a perfect beach
Kiwi fruits,
Sunset and paradise.

Margaret Weir (14)
St Leonards School, St Andrews

HER JOURNEY

She beats her wings,
Feeling the faint flutter,
Of a contented life
Slowly drift away.

She remembers the warm
Comforting cocoon, then awakening
To the fresh spring breeze
As she broke loose from her crystal cage.

Her first flight as she opened her
Expanse of wing.
Seeing the sun, hit
Upon that wondrous golden dust
She trailed behind her
Blessing everything she touched.

That first taste of the sweet, sweet nectar
From her favourite berry tree
Once at sunrise, catching a glimpse of herself in a glistening dewdrop
And understanding why we creatures stare in awe.

With the last beat of her upper wing
She falls among the leaves,
At one with nature and herself.

Kirstie Ferguson (16)
St Leonards School, St Andrews

THE END OF THE BEGINNING

Your first gasp of newborn air,
Your first tuft of golden hair,
Your first light, your first dark,
Your first trip to the park,
Your first disappointment,
Your first lie,
Your first proper giggle,
Your first proper cry,
Your first life, your first death,
Your first chocolate bar theft,
Your first party, your first kiss,
You never knew life would be like this.

Your first pressure, your last exam,
Your first date, your first man,
Your first marriage, your last divorce,
Your first newborn, your first Porsche,
Your last celebration, your last gift,
You're starting to need to use the lift,
Your last view of your grandchildren's smiles,
Your last glance at those grotty kitchen tiles,
Your last rock in our grandmother's chair,
Your last cuddle from your favourite bear,
Your first trip to the hospital beds,
Your first time of being dead.

Lucinda Barton (12)
St Leonards School, St Andrews

FLASHBACK

Hazy eyes.
Spinning walls.
Blurred lights.
Distant voices.
She's back in time.
Trapped.
The sweet sea air is sickening.
The sounds of crashing waves flood her mind.
Fear seeping through every vein in her body;
Like a fever in the darkness.
A great welling up of dread threatens to suffocate.
An abiding anguish.
Rain falls from the sky and clouds fill her palpitating heart.
Cold is the wind biting through her.
Frozen is her face.
Frozen in a state of sadness that will never leave.
A torrent of lamentation.
Familiar colours return on comforting walls.
She's back in reality, her visit is over.
Huddling in bed she searches for comfort,
Exuding her sadness through a muffle of covers.
Completely lost in a reverie of terror.
The window traps her reflection,
Revealing her white mask of guilt.
Hard, cold eyes stare back at her.
The eyes of pain.
They have seen and been through much.
She can see through them just as they can see through the glass.
Rain falls from her eyes
As she looks into the glass, she looks into her soul.
But there it is not so clear
It is clouded by hatred.

Hatred for life's little lessons, only taught by painful experiences.
A trance of irresolution.
The pulse of hopeful life is no longer warm,
In her empty space, like a hole in the sky.

Holly Curless (15)
St Leonards School, St Andrews

JOURNEY TO JANETTA'S

Our lunch is done,
Our money in hand,
We glance at our watches,
And nervously stand.

Now, we're all here,
Let's have some fun!
It's getting late though,
We might need to run.

Look both ways and cross the street,
A streak of green skirts and running feet.

We have arrived,
But hurriedly pick,
Bags of sweeties,
And things to lick.

We pay our fee,
And take a bite.
Someone shouts: 'Three minutes!'
And we're out of sight!

Collapse into seats, finally here,
The bell rings for class. Nothing to fear.

Emily McSwain (12)
St Leonards School, St Andrews

JOURNEYS

Travelling through the infinity of space
Time unmetered, gravity unchecked
Diamond drops fill the sky
Circular moons hang in mid-air.

Once a strange and distance place
Known by man, known by all
One time, one zone
A place so far from home.

Gliding through forever
Jupiter, Mars, Venus and Saturn
Journeying through time and space
A distant race, a distant place
The journey continues.

Natalie Stevenson (16)
St Leonards School, St Andrews

JOURNEYS

Moving forward,
Moving back,
Twisting, turning, surprises round every corner.

Walking the unknown paths,
Treading in the old footsteps,
Spinning, wheeling, never knowing where to turn.

Paths forking, choices made
Life's many adventures
You never know what's next.

Never knowing what to expect.

Samantha Evans (14)
St Leonards School, St Andrews

COMPARISON

Your life to a journey,
The journey to a road,
A hill to climb,
An avalanche bringing you down
Preventing you from reaching your goal,
A rock, a tree helping you on your way up
For the second time.

Does the road start at birth,
End at death?
Or is the 'journey' never-ending?
No beginning,
No end.

Clara Nelson Strachan (13)
St Leonards School, St Andrews

JOURNEY THROUGH LIFE

My essence is life
The essence of life is love
Love lives forever.

Complicate my thoughts
Twist them, turn them upside down
Then you can know me.

Does this ever end?
The game of life that we play
Or do the rules change?

Misinterpreted
Is the story of my life
Do you understand?

Georgina Greer (16)
St Leonards School, St Andrews

JOURNEY THROUGH THE YEAR

The journey begins,
Old snow on the floor.

Starting to melt,
As March opens its door.

Snowdrops appear,
Birds start to sing.

New lambs are born,
Joyous signs of spring.

Easter celebrations,
April and May.

Flowers in bloom,
New lambs play.

June, July, August,
Sun high in the sky.

Long lazy days,
Hot and dry.

Summer draws to a close,
Tractors loaded with grain.

September mists,
Autumn rain.

Leaves change to orange,
And fall to the ground.

Ghosts and ghouls scare,
Catherine wheels spin around.

Snow comes with December,
Crisp, white and cold.

Everybody celebrates, young and old,
With the New Year.

Comes the journey's end,
But now a new journey starts again.

Rosie Campbell Adamson (14)
St Leonards School, St Andrews

A WITHERING LEGACY

The summer sun sinks lower in the empty sky,
A smouldering hollow of ageing auburn,
Nights growing colder in the absence of her warmth.
The once vibrant woodland retreats
Ahead of the bitter months to come,
Nestling under a thick new covering of
Sunburnt leaves, a luscious blanket
To retain the sensuous glow of season's past.

Far up in the heavens
The itinerant birds make haste,
Sensing a growing urgency to be gone,
Leaving their skeleton homes
Now so stripped of their former lustre.
The first fledglings flit their fatherlands, brother and
Sister alike embarking on a sombre pilgrimage,
They chase the summer sun to her winter bed,
Challenging her in a race
To the bronzed depths of the southern sphere.

The tree-clad haunt is left deserted,
A withering legacy of what has gone before
It dares the creeping frost alone.
A sombre yet defiant picture remains,
Resolved to hazard the winter unaccompanied.

Natasha Briant-Evans (15)
St Leonards School, St Andrews

As Far As The Eye Can See

Memory is free to eat away at the future
As far as the eye can see
This road is long and absence is tender
But would it work for me?

While you sleep the moon will look watchful
Hearing the thoughts of soft dreams
The ones that meddle with crying hearts saying:
To forever love by all means.

Never be afraid of the path that's ahead
If like me you want to learn
You told me you don't need the comfort with it
So don't make it your concern.

Age could put all glory to doubt
But luck and logic sustains it
And in the places where it's alive and intense
Disabilities can always restrain it.

Why are you suddenly silent child?
Has the innocence in you been exposed?
While your heart is being lulled asleep,
Shut the door and keep it closed.

Memory is free to eat away at the future
As far as the eye can see
This road is long and absence is tender
But will it work for me?

Melanie Brechin (14)
St Leonards School, St Andrews

DREAM

A calm end to an endless day
A journey perhaps, a foreign land
Away to the ocean with wings of a bird.

Wings. A journey. East.

Verdant, yet unfamiliar, soaring high
Scented air and heavy with what
Spices, with herbs, with heat.

Wings. A journey. South.

Dry and dark, a precious land
Night birds in chorus serenade the silence
Living surroundings, yet acrid.

Wings. A journey. West.

Towering mountains, imposing, powerful
Uninhabited now but haunted by
A people long lost, forgotten.

Wings. A journey. North.

Incomparable beauty, untouchable ice,
Nothing but tangible solitude,
Unforgiving cold forces return.

Wings. A journey. Home.

An arrival, an awakening, another day
Till the night returns with sleep close by
My wings are clipped: I cannot fly.

Thea Stewart (16)
St Leonards School, St Andrews

SAME DESTINATION

The journey of life,
The way I see it
Everyone lives but some people
Appreciate it too much.

Some float through life
Accepting only what they feel they should
No bad occasions
Just to be happy.

Some are frantic
They panic and storm through the time they have
Not wanting to waste a second
Always waiting for new exciting lives.

We all have one life to live
Philosophy, the meaning of life
In the end there is still no answer,
In the end we all reach the same destination.

Lesley Coyle (16)
St Leonards School, St Andrews

REVERENCE

A melodramatic cloud
The essence of those nights
Knowing not what is to follow,
Fruitless anticipation persists.

Thus, it's the season of bundled
Hidden people
Searching in vain for times worthy
Of admiration.

Moods much different to our happy-go-lucky months,
Now upon us lie tense bitter ones
Lingering just long enough
To force appreciation from us.

Ivey Balderson (17)
St Leonards School, St Andrews

I REMEMBER

I remember the wind swept past my ears
Cold and fast.
Sea salt that tasted like tears
A moment that would never last.

I remember the sun that set was like a dream,
Heat turning cold.
Pink, orange, mauve and cream,
The day that was now old.

I remember the boat rocked so gently
Up and down.
I heard splashing sounds faintly
Near no cities, streets or towns.

I remember arriving in the dock,
Steady and slow.
Latches released for the unlock
We are free to go.

I remember jumping from the boat
Into my father's arms.
He wraps me in his coat
As we walk away, hand in hand, palm to palm.

Jessica Ventress (16)
St Leonards School, St Andrews

THE JOURNEY TO THE AIRPORT

It was summer,
It was hot,
It was only one day until the journey,
I hadn't even packed.

It's here, the journey
I packed my toothbrush,
My sponge and my hairbrush,
My clothes and my camera.

It was only five minutes until take-off
We all piled into the car,
Drove to the airport,
Now we are here.

Through the check in,
Up the stairs,
Through the x-ray
And on the plane.

We are here,
At last,
We made it,
The journey to the airport.

Poppy Lansdown (13)
St Leonards School, St Andrews

THE SKI RACE

Whoosh down the slope,
Won't fall I hope.
Through the first gate,
Just look at me skate.
Wind through my hair,
As downwards I tear.

Fifth gate is near,
When I have a sudden fear.
Over a bump,
Just look at me jump.
Phew that was close,
Oh no . . a post!
. . . ahhhh!

Jenny Cuthbert (15)
St Leonards School, St Andrews

THE MONSTER JOURNEY

The green and purple one-eyed monsters,
Emigrate to the Land of Lobsters.
They travel in a long line, single file,
They don't tire, walking mile after mile.

Spiders stare in the morning light,
For they have seen a bizarre sight.
But the procession of monsters do not care,
They think, just let them stare.

We're going to Lobster Land
We're escaping to the drier sand.
Soon we'll be at Lobster Camp
Away and out of this dismal damp.

The big monsters crawl to their destination,
To the lobster infestation.
The monster journey comes to an end,
But the lobsters can't pretend that,

They consider these colourful beasts,
From the land in the east,
A disturbance to their lobster peace.

Genny Hippisley (15)
St Leonards School, St Andrews

THE SETTLERS

Dusty, dusty wagons,
Rolling across the plain.
The settlers inside them,
Rarely see the rain.

The horses' coats are matted,
With dung and thorns and clay.
The smell would really knock you down
So you'd better stay away.

The men are all big strapping lads,
As villainous as scum.
Although they're skilled in what they do,
They all are rather dumb.

Before them many have come this way,
And many more will follow.
To seek a better life elsewhere
And leave behind their sorrow.

Benjamin Lisle (13)
St Leonards School, St Andrews

MY HOLIDAY

It's time to go
I can hardly wait
It's two o'clock
We mustn't be late.

As the plane takes off
Children start to cry.
They soon settle down
When we're high in the sky.

As the plane descends
I'm filled with excitement
'Only five minutes till landing'
Says the pilot's announcement.

We finally arrived
And got off the plane
My holiday was great
But now we're home again.

Susanna Pettigrew (15)
St Leonards School, St Andrews

THE BLACK DRAGON

Talons scraping off the ground,
It made the most awful sound,
Ready for take off, full of face,
Up we went, with no care,
Soon I was flying through the air,
With the most enormous wings,
In the sky you see many things,
The journey quickened just a notch,
If I fell my body would go splotch!
Its body, smooth for all the scales,
We landed by a catwalk of rails,
As I climbed off his scaly back
His beautiful colour of deep black,
Even though I had a lot of fun
I'm really glad the journey's done.

Jamie McInnes (13)
St Leonards School, St Andrews

BIG FIELD

The hands of time go round the face
At the speed of a howling gale.
Red-faced, we charge round the corner
Hockey boots clattering on the concrete slabs.

'You're late!'

The clock chimes
We find ourselves half way round,
Sticks 'ready fallen softly to the ground.
I falter, my bright blue socks are
No longer at my knees.
I stoop but:

'No!'

The voice races across the grass:

'Run!'

Nearly there, I stumble, try to carry on.
The sound of heavy breathing comes close,
Passes with a breathless shout.

I see the bucket, retrieve my hockey stick.
The journey is over but the labour has just begun.
I whack a fluorescent ball.
Then I have to:

'Run!'

Sarah Fleming (13)
St Leonards School, St Andrews

THE GOLF BALL

I am a golf ball
Just one of them
Every now and then
I'm pulled out of the bag
Today's the day
Out I come
Placed on a tee
Ready for action
With a name
And a number
I'll never get lost
A swish
Then a swoop
I'm off
Up to the sky
Higher and higher
I'm starting
To slowly descend
Closer and closer
To the ground
Oh no
This place is jaggy and thick
I can't see
Anybody or anything
I hear laughing
And talking
But nobody
Is coming to get me
It has all gone quiet
Not even a footstep.
I am a golf ball,
I am lost.

Stewart Mackenzie-Shaw (13)
St Leonards School, St Andrews

THE LONGEST JOURNEY EVER!

Come gather round my children all
Let me tell you a tale not *so* tall,
I tell you of a journey
The longest journey ever!

Two men set off from where we are,
To go to Brazil in their car
On the M6 they did go,
But it was very slow.

They now went to a land called Wales,
And behind a bus were slower than snails,
It was dark and very cold,
So in a hotel they did hold.

The next day they ventured out
And when the roads were blocked they did shout,
They took the bridge over the Severn
And on the cycle path, it wasn't Heaven.

So our gallant heroes arrive,
At the busy, noisy hive,
That we call Bristol, in our way
But their friends were away!

Miranda Butler (12)
St Leonards School, St Andrews

A CHILD IS BORN

A child is born,
Another dies, one begins, another ends,
Through days of tantrums of despair
And pulling out soft baby hair.

Then onto questions, why this and why that,
Why do I have to wear that hat?
Nobody listens and nobody cares,
I really need that talking bear.

Sometimes happy, sometimes sad,
Trying to fit in without being bad,
Different choices, what do I choose?
One way or another I am sure to loose.

I have decided, but still have doubts,
My family, my job, unwanted shouts,
I know my priorities and my duties,
Even though some are far from beauties!

A child is born, another dies,
My journey is over, my choices are made,
I always look back and wish I had stayed,
Where I wanted instead of being different,
And hoping to please -
My journey could have been one of ease.

Sarah Hartland-Mahon (13)
St Leonards School, St Andrews

A JOURNEY TO THE MOON

'10, 9, 8, 7, 6, 5, 4, 3, 2, 1,
Lift off'
Are the last words you hear,
When you blast into space,
Not a word of comfort,
Like you might prefer,
But a stranger's voice on the tannoy,
Telling you it's time to go,
You can't change your mind
At the last minute or second
You can't shout 'Stop'
Like you could in your dream.

If you need the loo it has to wait,
If you don't want to go it's too late,
If you want to see your family,
You've missed your chance,
You can't stop the rocket it's too late,
You've made the decision and can't change now!

'Stop' a little voice says in your head
'I don't want to go
I want to see my wife, kids, family.
I might never see them again.'
But it's too late.

Nicola Montague (13)
St Leonards School, St Andrews

A Journey To A Better Place

Everybody has a place where they long to be,
A place where you feel tranquil,
A place where you feel free,
Somewhere free,
From war, destruction, poverty.

Some may have this place,
Maybe there everyday,
But others are in a different place,
Where they slave away.
Where just from drinking water,
They have debts to pay.

These people, these unfortunates,
Dream of journeys far away,
Anywhere but there,
In the sweating, humid air,
Where death, instant like a telephone call,
And every hour's unfair.

They suffer every second,
With no drink, no food to eat,
But they journey to a better place,
Every time they go to sleep.

Kirsten Donaldson (13)
St Leonards School, St Andrews

STROMA

The island was dark,
There was one basking shark
Circling around Stroma.
A blinding flash, a lightning dash
Lit up the shores of Stroma.

A ship appeared,
The inhabitants feared
That she would not reach Stroma
For a storm was blowing and the people knowing
What would happen that night on Stroma.

The ship sailed on,
But soon was gone,
She had crashed into the side of Stroma.
One girl survived. Oh how she cried
There on the shores of Stroma.

And to this day
Some people say
She haunts the shores of Stroma
Wailing and calling, she seems to be falling
From the cliffs at Stroma.

Catriona Sinclair (12)
St Leonards School, St Andrews

TRAVEL AGENT

They pick up our brochure,
Say they're looking for a cure.

'After a romantic break,
Somewhere near a lake.'

'A week with the family,
In a B&B in Cranleigh.'

'Health course for Mum,
So she can lose her tum.'

'Looking for a gap year,
Not too far from here.'

'A villa in the sun,
Jam-packed full of fun.'

'Foreign exchange,
For a bit of a change.'

Then they look at the price,
Start to think twice.

Andrew Bradley (13)
St Leonards School, St Andrews

LIFE

As I walk,
I think of life
The things I've done
All so long ago.

Achievements,
Disappointments,
Through life's
Rough road.

From young to old
I will always recall,
Memories of past,
Hopefully of future.

I will always regret,
Some days of my life,
But I will always feel
I have lived life happily.

Now ninety-five,
My days are up
I feel life drying out of me
Not long to go.

I hope my grandchildren
Will have as happy
A life as me!

Katy Eccles (14)
St Leonards School, St Andrews

LIFE

I am waiting, waiting to be born,
Waiting for the moment for my life to begin,
The time for my existence has come.

I have lived through seven summers,
I have learnt more now then I shall ever learn,
How to read,
How to write,
How to speak,
How to use the language of emotions.

Now I have reached my teenage years,
I am in the years of adolescence,
I don't know what to do with my life,
I still think I am the greatest thing the world has ever seen,
But my life keeps changing for better and for worse.

That's it I have reached the big three - zero,
I am spoken for in marriage,
My children are learning the things I learnt.
I know what I want to do,
Live life to the full.

My life is coming to an end now,
My children now have children
My husband has departed from life, it is time for me to join him.

Today is the end.
The fullstop presence
I have lived through one jubilee
Four decades and five years.

I am waiting, waiting to die
Waiting for the moment for life to end
The time for my existence has ended.

Alyson Mckechnie (13)
St Leonards School, St Andrews

CYCLING

I've never been cycling,
But I'll give it a good bash,
I'm preparing for the worst,
I'm ready for a crash.

'Come on James! Get on the bike!
I'm not going to wait all day,'
Seeing him fall is what I'd like
But it's not quite worth the pay.

Wobble, wobble, wobble,
Ah! I'm going to fall,
My sister's going to get in trouble,
If I cycle into the wall.

She shouldn't have made me do this,
But hey, I haven't crashed,
I wish I knew how to stop though,
Uh! Oh! Smash!

Robert Torrance (13)
St Leonards School, St Andrews

THE CRASH THAT CHANGED AMERICA

Their pride and joy gone,
Thousands dead,
Millions mourn
It's always in the head.

The world looks on in horror,
With hatred and spite,
While we all ponder
What will happen and what next?

But their true colours show
They come together
What's happening? We don't know
It changes like the weather.

We trust them to do what's best,
We stick by them,
We don't care about the rest,
We *will* find who's to blame!

Carmen Murray (12)
Sanquhar Academy

BULLIES

They like to act so big and tall,
They like to smoke and drink,
If only for one moment
I wish they'd stop and think.

They pick on smaller children
The rules they don't obey
If only they would realise
They'll regret this all one day.

As frightened as a mouse is he
In a corner, out of the way
For if at once he does appear
He's a victim who is easy prey.

The scars he bears are deep inside
Scars that do not show
For all the hurt and pain he feels
The bully will not ever know.

Sarah Hughes (14)
Sanquhar Academy

CELEBRATIONS

You have one on a birthday
If you won the lottery,
A wedding reception is one,
But Christmas is the greatest
And a funeral the worst
Although it celebrates a person's life.
We should all celebrate the highs and lows
This being because life is short
So enjoy it and celebrate when you can!

Sarah Allan (12)
Sanquhar Academy

STRANRAER

S   is for sea horses and Southern Upland Way,
    we also get sunshine every single day.
T   is for teatime, we eat lots of food, so go to one of our restaurants,
    they are really good.
R   is for rum, we do like our drink, so go to our pubs and have a pint.
A   is for animals, there's plenty about, but from what I've noticed
    none have foot and mouth.
N   is for night time, the starlight is nice, so why don't you go out
    and have a romantic night.
R   is for reality it's all very real, it may be beautiful but it's definitely
    not a dream.
A   is for academy, it's a good, big school, there's plenty of classes
    and that's for real.
E   is for enjoyment, you get it by going into the country
    and having a good time.
R   is for Rhins of Galloway, it is the place to be every day,
    so once again I will say, come on down to the Rhins of Galloway.

Iain Govan (11)
Stranraer Academy

A LOAD OF LIMERICKS

There was a young boy from Portpatrick,
Who played football and scored a hat-trick.
He scored one with his nut,
And two with his butt.
Now he's McLaren's first choice pick.

There was a young boy from Stranraer,
Who had a shiny rock guitar.
He played it all day
And scared the neighbours away.
Now he is a great rock 'n' roll star.

There was a golfer from Creachmore,
Who lost a ball on the shore.
He hit a gull's head,
And knocked it stone dead.
Next time he's gonna shout 'Fore.'

There was a farmer from Palnure,
Who had the finest cow manure.
Out it would come,
From every cow's bum.
Without a doubt it was pure.

Gillian Monteith (11)
Stranraer Academy

FOOTBALL

Fans in the stands,
Opposition's taking their places,
Fans are shouting for their team
The ball is in the back of the net
The fans are cheering!

Alison Knox (11)
Stranraer Academy

THE SEA

The sea has two faces
A rough one, a calm one
It churns up the water
Like a liquidiser
Next comes a tidal wave.

The sea has two faces
Which come and go
It throws boats around
Like a child playing with a toy
Many people have died in the current.

The sea has two faces
You cannot predict them
But when it's nice
The water is warm and fresh
What a nice day at the beach.

The sea has two faces
Most people don't mind
When it's sunny and warm
And the sea is calm
But for how long?

Stephen Anderson (12)
Stranraer Academy

THE CAT

The night was dark, the wind was still,
I saw a cat on my window sill.
Its eyes were shining very bright
Like burning orange candlelight.

Its whiskers twitched, its teeth were bare,
I looked again, it was not there.
Where or why did it go?
I suppose now I'll never know!

Shani McColm (13)
Stranraer Academy

MY GRIEF

Thousands of people have died,
I grieved for weeks afterwards
For them? Yes
For me? Yes.

I cry when I think of the people who died,
The fear in their hearts,
Their families,
The endless posters of missing people,
Husbands, wives, mums, dads, brothers, sisters.

I grieve when I think of the retaliation,
What's to come?

I had ambitions, hopes, and dreams,
They were shattered like the buildings.
Part of my life is now fear.
I fear what's to come,
I'm scared to look too far forward.

It's a selfish reaction, I know,
Selfish but natural.
I fear I lose what many have lost all ready,
My life!

Emma Hughes (13)
Stranraer Academy

MY NIECE

The first time I saw you, your eyes sparkling bright,
The first time I held you, you were wrapped up so tight.
I helped to bath you and feed you your lunch
And made up your bottle so that you could munch.

You started to crawl and were eating some food
You were so cute and really good.
We played with your toys and had such fun
It'll not be long until you're starting to run.

And sure enough you started to walk
Crawling round furniture, starting to talk,
Wanting books read to you,
Wanting more fed to you,
And now you're so tall, not any more small
I love you, my niece, I love you so much.
I love you, my niece, I hope we never lose touch.

Debbie Muirhead (14)
Stranraer Academy

THE SKY

All over, all around
The bright blue sky above
So like a sheet of silk
And shines all day and night.

All over, all around
The black, thundering sky above
Lightning flashing, thunder rumbling,
The sky is so alive.

All over, all around,
The stars glistening so beautifully
The moon brightens up the sky
And is alight, all around us.

Emma Skilling (13)
Stranraer Academy

NEW YORK SKY

Standing below I look up at the New York sky
I see the Twin Towers soaring high.
I look across and see a plane flying low
And suddenly the towers sway to and fro.
Then I hear the screams and shouts and cries
And I see the concrete and glass as it flies.
As I walk through the ruins of what used to be
Thousands of people are trapped under me.
Then I hear a voice through all the commotion
A voice choking on dust and emotion.
I try and I try to sieve my way through
As I fight through the dust that we all once knew.
I turn and I watch tearful strangers on streets
Comforting each other and people they meet.
This tragedy brings them together, yet tears them apart
Who could do this and why? They can't have a heart.
In under an hour everything changed
These monsters who did this - what have you gained?
You silenced our world in just one day
But we'll get revenge and you shall pay!
Standing below I look up at the New York sky
I see clouds of dust billowing high.

Victoria Parker (15)
Stranraer Academy

THE SKY

The sky was a bright, blue like a crystal clear sea,
It looked like silk but fragile to me.
The pure blue, glistening sky
While no wind passed me by.

The next day the sky was blue with fluffy white clouds
It reminded me of sheep floating around in the sparkling, blue sea
They were slowly swaying, swinging softly with the waves,
While a small breeze of wind passed over me.

The following day the sky was a bright shimmer of pink,
Like a sunset on the horizon on a lovely calm day.
But I knew it wouldn't last forever.
The skies would burst and blast down rain.
While a calm, smooth and gentle wind passed over me.

The next day the sky was a dull grey,
Like tearful eyes on a poor child's face,
The heavens broke into a thunderstorm with bangs and flashes that
frightened me.
While a wild gale of wind pushed violently passed me.

Karen Copeland (12)
Stranraer Academy

GOLF

I swing my club back and forth
Oops a daisy it's on the fourth.
I hit my next shot, boy it's glorious
But ooh no, it's starting to pour on us.
I was getting good at this game
Until this horrible, stupid rain!

Hugh Parker (12)
Stranraer Academy

THE NY DISASTER

Planes flying really high
Up above in the sky.
Terrorists took over the planes
And made the people die.

President has announced that
We are at war with those clowns
They took our twin towers
And now we are going to get them
Back with our powers.

Many people died
And many people cried.
Only a few survived.
This tragic and hurtful event
Caused this terrible conflict.

Stacey Lees (14)
Stranraer Academy

THE SHOWS

Twenty pounds cash,
To the shows I dash.

Music's blaring, vibes are thumping,
On the tagada I'm jumping.

My money is spent in half an hour
Thank God I spent it
Here's a shower.

Home I go, it's half-past ten,
Oh no I'm grounded once again.

Ally Muir (11)
Stranraer Academy

WHICH IS THE LION AND WHICH IS THE KING?

He silently creeps among the crowd,
Making sure he is not spotted,
Choosing his victims with care,
Preparing to pounce on the unsuspecting.
His bloodthirsty mind plots how to make his kill.
His steady eye surveys his subjects.
His blue blood could overpower any,
As could his crown, his mane.
As quick as a flash, his mind racing,
He picks his body off the ground.
His superiority has already won
The monarch's decision is made.
Which is the lion and which is the king?

Daniel Squair (12)
Stranraer Academy

AUBURN AUTUMN

Brown, orange, yellow and red
Colours of autumn, summer is dead.
Leaves are gently falling down
Swaying like feathers to the ground.

A glimmer of light across the pond,
As autumn waves its magic wand.
Hibernation it will creep,
Hedgehogs begin their long, long sleep.

Leaves are dancing all around,
A cosy carpet upon the ground,
Darkness falls, the night grows long,
Nocturnal noises, like an evening song.

Gayle Mitchell (12)
Stranraer Academy

NIGHT

Night is spooky, eerie and dark
You might even hear some dogs bark
There're weird things that happen in the night
Don't go out or you might get a fright.

The wind howling in the night
Better be careful or you'll end up with a bite
So keep out of sight
Don't go out or you might get a fright.

Branches tapping at your window
The rain beating down on the street
By this time you can't get to sleep
Don't go out or you might get a fright.

Stephanie Ward (12)
Stranraer Academy

THE TOWERS

One still, calm day
Whilst we were working away.
There came from the distance disaster and pain
Inflicted upon us by the human insane
The sudden explosion of terror and death
As people tried to escape from the crumbling mess
Then all of a sudden the buildings came down
The peak of man's power crushed to the ground
The shock, the horror of a world united in grief
Oh why, oh why, can we not live in peace?

Ashley Williamson (12)
Stranraer Academy

TWIN TOWERS

They stood proud and erect,
Towering towards the sky.
A landmark building,
Amongst others not so high.

Full of working people,
At the start of a September's day.
Unaware of the terror,
Coming their way.

They came from above,
In the shape of a plane.
And in the explosions,
Few were to remain.

The buildings shook,
Fires raged all around.
Then horror upon horror,
The towers collapsed to the ground.

Twisted metal, piled high,
Debris-strewn streets.
Now the towers are gone,
Manhattan weeps.

The world awaits,
A war has begun.
The terrorists will be beaten,
And the war will be won.

Shona McClintick (12)
Stranraer Academy

HIM

This creature, this man
You thought you all knew
You don't know him at all, you ain't got a clue.

He puts up a front, as the family man
You all believe him, it's part of his plan.
Nobody sees him, he's not what you think,
He's pushed her to the edge, right over the brink.
Her mum turns a blind eye, not sure what to do.
Never tries to stop him, pays for him and his crew.
Down at his local, he's likely to be found,
You can't get him to leave, he'll always stand his ground.
When he's 'done in' enough, he'll eventually come home
She's surrounded by family, but she feels all alone.
They're told to be quiet, just to let him sleep,
She's scared and frightened, feelings she knows she'll keep.
He wakes up next day, expects them to forget
But it won't go away, the memories are set.
She'll forever be haunted, by memories of this man
She tries to move on, but doesn't think she can.
He doesn't let others, let them see what he's done,
She knows it would shame him, spoil his fun.
This man he says he gives her, all that she never had,
But you can't buy happiness, he must think she's mad.
She'll never ever forget, this feeling so sad
Set in her mind, by the man she calls dad.

This creature, this man
You thought you all knew,
You don't know him at all, you ain't got a clue.

Debbie Clegg (14)
Stranraer Academy

THE THING

What's that Thing that blows in my ear, my face, my body?
It is cold but refreshing, powerful but calm.
It flies through my hair, making it wavy and coarse.
It tickles my whole body, my arm, my palm.
It's the Thing, the Thing!

The Thing is something that is unseen by the human eye
But why when it hits me hard, I cannot see?
Does the Thing do this to me when it is angry? But why?
But what can it be? Oh yes . . .
It's the Thing, the Thing!

The Thing is gentle, wonderful and calm
It finds its way quietly down the alleys and streets.
But when the Thing is angry, it can be powerful and strong.
It can crumble everything, whatever it meets. But what is it?
It's the Thing, the Thing!

The Thing is gentle but so strong you might not believe this is true
The Thing can tickle a baby or destroy a whole tree.
So what is it that can do all of these things? Oh wait . . .
I know what it is. Why did I not get it before? How silly of me.
It's the Thing, the Thing!

Ryan Alexander (13)
Stranraer Academy

FOOTBALL POEM

Here we go! Here we go!
Here we go to Ibrox Stadium
With fans crowding around in a heap
Here we go! Here we go!

We're 3-0 up with fifteen minutes to go
The fans are shouting 'We're simply the best
We're winning 3-0 against Celtic.'
The full-time whistle has just blown,
Goal!

Grant Campbell-Gibson (13)
Stranraer Academy

DOLPHINS

Dolphins are mammals
That live in the sea
They are clever
Like you and me.

They swim in pods
So they're not alone
They hunt together
Far from home.

They swoop and dive
And sometimes float;
And sometimes pop up
Beside fishing boats.

They swim out in front
To show the way
Jumping and diving
As they play.

They swim along,
Even in the dark,
And if they need to,
They can kill a shark.

Debbie Ferries (14)
Stranraer Academy

THE FINAL FEW SECONDS

My final few gasps of fresh air
It has been many years since the wind blew through my hair
If this is my final breath
I hope it is a painless death.

Many times have I been ill
But this time I have had to write my will
I know my family love me so
So as my family remember me
I know where my possessions must now go.

Now I must get ready for my trip to that place in the sky
I put on my wings and prepare to fly.
If this time I finally die
At least - at least this time I have said goodbye.

Thomas Lindsay (14)
Stranraer Academy

STRANRAER

Stranraer is full of shops, it's well protected by the cops.
There's loads of clubs and loads of pubs and there's
                              even the Boy Scouts called the Cubs.
Stranraer has got lots of flowers, it also has lots of towers.
Stranraer is a peaceful place, its beauty hits you in the face.
So come and see it for yourself, do not leave us on the shelf.

Rebecca Harvey (12)
Stranraer Academy

THE EDIBLE KILL

Hat, shirt, trousers, shoes,
Sonny's real pit barbecue,
Hackle, cackle, hackle, cackle
Whose cattle have you crackled?
Days in, days out,
Piggy's got a lucky shout,
The door is open,
The road is clear
It's time for piggy to overcome his fear.
Angels, angels, angels of the animals
If animals were human,
We'd all be cannibals!

Elaine Scobie (15)
Stranraer Academy

CARTOONS

C artoons
A re
R eally
T remendous
O ld
O riginals but
N ever
S tale.

Scott Campbell (12)
Stranraer Academy

BEHIND THE EYE

As I look
Look into a face
Of anger, sorrow
And disbelief.

I imagine
Imagine what it feels
How it feels
To only see
Half of a world,
Half of a life,
Half of everything.

As I stare
Stare into the eye
The eye of
Hope and discomfort
Thoughts of life
And
Memories
Good and bad
Fill a tear
A tear
That falls
Falls from a face of sadness.

Tracey Marr (14)
Stranraer Academy

CHIMNEY SWEEP

Up and down the ladder
With a bag and brush in hand.
I clean those dirty chimneys
The best I can.

I like to think I'm helping
To stop that awful soot.
From causing chimney fires
And making lots of loot.

Harry Rothmund (13)
Stranraer Academy

THE SEASONS

Blowing through trees' leaves
Falling to the ground
With all its colour around.

Snowflakes fall and softly
Hit the ground
Soon there's whiteness
All around.
Winter is upon us
With all its colour and glory.

Daffodils flower in the cold
Birds sing melodies in the trees
As leaves unfold.
Spring is upon us
With all its colour around.

Golden sun shines
It's light on the sandy beaches
Summer is upon us
With all its warmth and sun.

Justin Kassell (13)
Stranraer Academy

HATE

Why do men show so much hate
And twist the winding road of fate?
Who gives them the right of power
To bring down any tower?

As Bush and Blair push more and more
The blood will now begin to pour
And now they've decided on their date
Why do men show so much hate?

The death bell now shall toll
For Blair and Bush are in a hole
So what gives a few angry men power
To bring down any tower?

If war persists, you will many hear groans
As more and more people lose their homes.
Soon we shall see so much gore
As Bush and Blair push more and more.

Bombs will fill the skies like showers
It shall go on for many hours
Why do men twist the road of fate?
Why do men show so much hate?

Mothers and children shall wail
As fathers and husbands faces turn pale
People in the streets shall fall
The death bell now shall toll.

These two sides will not agree
Not even to a certain degree
Who gives a man as much power
To destroy so much in around an hour?

How can a few non-specific men
Bring us to what could be the end?

Emma Horberry (12)
Stranraer Academy

THE WEATHER

On a day when the sun shines down,
We like to go down town,
To look in shops, sometimes spending lots,
On a day when the sun shines down.

On a day when the rain falls down,
We don't go down town,
We don't look in shops, we don't spend lots,
On a day when the rain falls down.

On a day when the wind blows high,
Blowing the leaves off all the trees,
On a day when the wind blows high,
Dying to a breeze.

On a night when the snow falls down,
Laying softly on the ground,
The lights all round, feet making a crunching sound,
On a night when the snow falls down.

It's all to disappear, it's the start of a brand new year
Weather shall change, people shall not, they'll all stand and cheer
They shall brave the weather, rain, wind, sunshine or snow
Whatever to be, from day to day, we do not really know.

David Stanage (12)
Stranraer Academy

WHY?

Why are they staring?
Haven't they seen me before?
I'm here every day, why only just notice me now?
But I suppose today has been a bit strange,
I mean it's not as cold as it was last night.
Last night was so cold, I sat still, afraid
To move for fear of losing what precious little bit
Of heat my lifeless body produced.

There's John! He's one of the few people
Who say hello.
'Hi John' I call out as he passes by my spot.
He ignores me!
Why did he do that?
I tried to reassure myself that he was busy.
I think consolingly to myself that he will
Work himself into an early grave.
I laugh silently to myself.

But that doesn't answer my question
Why do I feel different? I address this question
To no one.
My random thoughts race back to the night before
Though they soon hit an icy cold blackness.
Just as I did.

Why can't I remember?
Why don't I remember?
Why do I feel warm?
What has happened to the bitter cold that bit
And enveloped me on previous nights?

Suddenly the rust ridden door behind me creaked
Open on its iced hinges
I look up expecting to receive the usual icy glare.
I receive nothing
Why doesn't he look back?

Laura Allison (15)
Stranraer Academy

THE WEATHER

Whoosh go the winds
Flattening all the hay
Leaves are flying off the trees
Looks like I'll not be going out today.

Drip, drop goes the rain
Outside in the garden it lay
The road is now a river
Looks like I'll not be going out today.

Bang goes the thunder
I'm too scared to play
Flashes of lightning come around
Looks like I'll not be going out today.

The sun is shining down at me
Hip, hip hooray!
It's nice and warm
I'm going outside to play.

William Hurcomb (13)
Stranraer Academy

MY PUPPY

He's just a little puppy
Small and black
With big floppy ears
And a white spot on his back.

He liked to go walking
Day and night
And at night-time especially
Because he can chase the torch light.

He chased the cats
And the hens too
Sometimes I think
He thought he was in a zoo.

He liked egg and milk for breakfast
And biscuits and meat for tea
And then we'd take him for his walk
So he could have a dip in the sea.

Stacey Cathro (13)
Stranraer Academy

NIGHT

Darkness is falling,
Owls are calling,
Foxes are prowling,
The wind is howling,
The moon is shining,
Giving each cloud a silver lining,
Stars are glistening,
As I lie listening,
To all the sounds of night.

Fiona MacPherson (13)
Stranraer Academy

MY SCHOOL BUS

My school bus is an old school bus
And everyone is always smoking
I think it's so sick
Often I feel like boaking.

When it goes over a hump
It makes a bang and a bump.

My school bus is not that nice
I've experienced that only being on it twice.

I would like a new school bus
That is nice and clean
Unlike this one that is ugly and mean.

I am nearing the end
My bus is driving me round the bend
And I hope nobody has this experience again.

John Morrison (12)
Stranraer Academy

FISHING DOWN BY THE RIVER

F   riendly people catching fish
I   s it going to take the bait?
S   illy people trying to catch
H   iding behind the weed at the bottom
I   n the boat, drifting along
N   othing jumping, getting bored
G   oing home with nothing for dinner.

Damien Young (12)
Stranraer Academy

COMBINED PROVINCES VS SOUTH AFRICA

Out came the two teams, strong and proud,
To the cheers of the support, which were very loud.
To the blow of the ref's whistle, it was some blast,
The game kicked off at Ravenhill, Belfast.

P. Hendricks caught the ball and to his dismay,
He was met with a thump by Michael Galwey.
Francis gave the Provinces quite a good spell,
And finally a try for Jonathan Bell.
The Provinces at half-time, up seven-nil,
You should have seen South Africa they looked really ill.

For South Africa he came on, Van Der Westhuizen,
He was up against number fourteen PJ Gavin.
South Africa scored a penalty,
The game was close, he scored, seven-three.

Five minutes left and South Africa knew,
Just exactly what to do.
A kick that went straight into touch,
Time was ticking, they didn't have much.

The Provinces caught and hoofed up the park,
Into the night sky, which was very dark.
The ref blew his whistle, the game was won,
And the Provinces had got the job done.

Patrick Balmer (14)
Stranraer Academy

WE'RE ON OUR WAY TO GLASGOW

Clunk, clunk, clunk,
What's that noise? It doesn't sound good
The car's not going as it should.
We are all packed up and ready to go
To take my sister back to Glasgow.
Further along the road the noise gets worse
Mum starts to worry (and even curse!)
'I can fill up with petrol,' says Mum in a panic
'But this is beyond me, we need a mechanic.'
'Where are you going?' shouts Kathryn 'Are you insane?'
As Mum signals right and turns up Park Lane.
We'll never make it to the top of the hill
And I start praying it will, it will.
We make it to the top of the hill and out at the top
And on past Lidl where my gran likes to shop.
We're going to Mirrey's to see Davy King
And with any luck he'll find this thing
That's causing us problems and giving us grief
We all wait patiently as he looks underneath.
'It's a stone,' he says as he slides back out.
Mum looks relieved and I give a shout.
He gives it the once over to check it's OK
And within ten minutes we're back on our way.

Gavin Kerr (14)
Stranraer Academy

YOU ARE IMPORTANT

In moments of doubts, you may say it aloud,
'I'm nobody special, a face in the crowd,
I won't be remembered for things that I've said,
I've little to show for the life that I've led.'
Well listen to me, get your head off your chest,
Don't judge your importance by fame and success,
You've set yourself standards and values of worth,
You're loved and considered the salt of the earth,
For the genuine feelings that set you apart,
And the caring affection that springs from your heart,
With the warmth and the wisdom
In the words that you speak,
These are the talents that make you unique,
Plus one added extra required of a star,
You're the last one to know
How important you are.

Naomi McCreadie (14)
Stranraer Academy

MY SPECIAL SISTER

She cares for me
In a very special way.
Smells a rat when there's something wrong,
Tells me all her secrets and I tell her mine,
Endlessly listening to me,
Reads my mind,
She's the best!

Alexa Kerr (14)
Stranraer Academy

LIFE

The day was no different
From any other day
Until it was over.

Thousands of people walked along
The street being pushed by the tide of people
Eight-forty-five, early again
We all crushed our insignificant
Bodies into the moving box
That was made for thirty
And crushed in sixty
Like a hundred cows in a small pen.

Ping, the doors opened and the human stampede started
Get caffeine and start work
That was everybody's aim.
Bang and a rush of heat flooded through the building
Followed by the clouding of smoke.

Screaming, shouting, running
Everybody trying to escape the terror.
Some jumped and some burned,
Then, silence . . . the building
Smashed into the ground
And every living soul in the building was lost.

Life, can end at any second . . .

Megan Kerr (16)
Stranraer Academy

MY BEST FRIEND

L auren is my best friend
A lways there for me
U nderstanding and caring
R eliable and sharing
E verlasting friendship
N o matter where she'll be.

Laura Herron (13)
Stranraer Academy

I WANT

I want some new trousers,
And a pair of new shoes.
I want a tuna sandwich,
And I want rid of the blues.
I want a squillion pounds,
So I could spoil all my friends
And I want the sound of laughter,
To follow me to the end.

I want to be amazing,
At everything I do.
I want to be wonderful,
And never catch the flu.
I want escalators,
To rid of all the stairs
And I want a fireworks display
With loads of rockets and flares.

I want to have my mates,
With me all the time
And as long as I have this
Everything will be fine!

Justine Fialka (13)
Tain Royal Academy

JOURNEY THROUGH DARKNESS

I'm in a tunnel
The end can't be seen
In front of me thick, black clouds swirl
They black out my future.

I know there is light
Yet behind me it lies,
And only in front can exist,
For at my back lies a wall, from which I can't escape.

Even though I can't see,
I know what is waiting,
Obstacles obstructing the path to the end,
And there lies fear itself.

A tall hooded figure,
Cruel as can be,
In his hand lies a thick pack of cards,
To be picked off, one by one.

What I fear is the end of the pack,
For I know what it means,
I cease to exist,
If only in dreams.

You can't change the past,
Or see the future,
Death is unexpected,
Do you want the tunnel to end?

Stuart Tennent (14)
Tain Royal Academy

JACK AND THE FAIRIES

Jack's eyes were red and all aflame,
When back through dreaded woods he came,
Where cry of wolf and eaters of men
Had lived long, near the fairy glen.
For long ago when he was small
His father took a nasty fall
And with no money for his care
His mother came and left him there.
The fairies went to steal the boy
And take him home for prince's toy
Crying and wailing he did come
To fairy glen unseen by some.
Loved by the prince he did grow
Underground, where time was slow.

Now Jack he was a merry fellow,
His nights were black; his days were yellow,
Until one day, when Jack saw
That he wasn't a fairy so lived not by their law.
So on a journey he was sent
To stay in the woods till he would repent
Jack went and saw a thousand things,
Biggilo bats and teeth and wings
Crying wolves with red, red eyes,
Banshees with their dreaded cries,
Day by day in terror spent,
But still Jack, he would not repent
He wandered far and home he strayed
To a rich mum with a pretty maid.
Jack fell in love and children had he
All fairy boys by age of three.

Ruth Cockshott (14)
Tain Royal Academy

THE STONE

Walking down this road
(I feel I'm walking in a picture)
The trees set high, lean over me like arches.

I stop
A stone, lies huge amongst the forest
Sitting near the fence undisturbed by man.

Brambles grow over it and green moss its coat,
But still its shape remains,
As if placed clearly within my mind's eye.

I feel something lies beneath, never to be revealed
Its nature, not warmed by human hands
It remains mindful of its limits.

When standing upon it, it centres me
With views from far around
Back through the woods I feel a heavy remorse
And pass the sucking stream.

Through the gates made up by two tall pines,
I can see home now covered by the clattering of leaves
I'll keep this stone a secret
(For as in a dream)
A panther lay beside it.

Tao Mackay (11)
Tain Royal Academy

WHY, OH WHY?

Why, oh why can the sky be so blue?
Why do clouds race along like that
From here to Timbuktu?

Why does lightning illuminate the sky so bright?
Why does thunder make such a loud
Noise without a sight?

Why do rainbows never finish up anywhere?
Why is the sun a bright, yellow sphere?

Why, oh why, oh why?
I've got so many questions about sky.

Tessa Budge (12)
Tain Royal Academy

FREEDOM

There is a final thump
And from the distance emerges a man
His face is bloody and torn, his eyes wrenched open
Dragging himself along the uneven track,
There is no one behind him
He is alone, alone except for the strong gates, a barrier,
He is reliving the screams, the helplessness,
The banging, the silence,
The sour taste of captivity
Yet, the smell of determination radiates
From his hollow body, through his tinged skin
And blood-stained armour,
Finally, he is free.

Stephanie Phillips (12)
Wallace High School

GOLF RULES - FOR BEGINNERS

A tense moment you're using your putter
Sometimes your hands feel just like butter,
You try to hit the ball as far as you can
You swing it, you smack it, pow wham!

Oh no the balls went into the rough
Into the weed grass and some other stuff.
I smack it, I give it my hardest shot
Oh my God, what a pot!

Lots of players get a par
That's mainly because they hit it far.
A bogey is bad, a birdie is good
Try to get your best score - everyone should.

Albatross, eagle, they're just normal words
In golf they have nothing to do with birds.
North, south, east and west
I think golf is the best.

Malcolm Gardiner (12)
Wallace High School

MY TEACHER

Like a monster dying to eat our heads.

Like a tiger ready to attack us.

Like a lion roaring all the time.

Like a manager when his team's getting beat at half-time.

Like a general when one of his men try and sneak away.

Ross Hilson (12)
Wallace High School

DEATH

What is death?
A thing that happens to all of us
Sooner or later,
Unexpected,
Accidents,
Murder,
Old age
Many people like death
It's a relief
Although there's a few
Who don't want it to come.
Either a skeleton in a cloak
With a scythe
Or a long tunnel
With a light at the end
This is death.

Liam Martin (12)
Wallace High School

A NEWSPAPER

A newspaper has razor-sharp teeth
They are fierce beasts
They bite people's shins
To get news from them.
They get them to write it in black and white
To be printed that night.
In millions we are made
We hit the early morning trade,
While the next day's news is being made.

Greg Paterson (13)
Wallace High School

THE SUN

The sun shines high,
Up in the big, blue sky
A big ball of fire
Glinting gold on the church spire.

People enjoy the sun
They can have lots of fun.
It helps the plants grow,
And takes away the snow.

Some people are always out with friends,
Building big, huge dens.
You make them from branches and sticks,
Making mud pies and of course bricks.

I like going to beaches and bays,
For a few days.
Going on holiday is fun
In the sun.

Emma Cairney (12)
Wallace High School

HALLOWE'EN

Hallowe'en is like the dark night, looking into the black sea,
Pumpkins in the windows and candles in the wind.
Witches rise from the dead like zombies in a trance
Ghosts flying about everywhere like sheet flying through the air.
The trick or treaters sing and dance like the Devil roaring and shouting.
The wind blows like a wolf howling.
As the clock strikes twelve the bells ring.
Zombies and devils fly away
They slip through the darkness like ghosts.

Caitlin Marshall (12)
Wallace High School

WORLD WRESTLING FEDERATION

The Rock will lay the smackdown
On your ass,
When you
Pass like a jackass.

The mood is about to change,
'Cause you are in his range,
Death never pounces on The Undertaker, in the dark,
British Bulldog's dog will bark.

The Rattlesnake will give and take
There is Y2J who you will obey
The Hardy Boyz who, no longer play with toys,
Heroes, all to me, with each fall and count of three.

The big show we cry for blood
To flow
The fans faces cheering. A fall from grace
Without a tear.

Scott Fishlock (12)
Wallace High School

A PARACHUTIST

Like a bomb dropping then exploding,
Like a bird soaring through the sky,
Like a big top being opened up,
Like a seed blowing in the wind,
Like a flower blooming in the sky,
Like a colourful rainbow,
Like a game that has to work,
Like a plane that has to land.

Robbie McGowan (12)
Wallace High School

MY CAT

Wearing a coat of ginger and white
Fur so smooth and silky
Gingery brown along his back
Underside white and milky.

Eyes sparkling like magic,
Gleaming vivid green,
Alert and alive at the slightest sound
Glowing at night, all to be seen.

Immaculate from nose to tail
Never a hair out of place
Nor speck of dirt visible
From his paws, his coat or face.

With gentle purrs and miaow sweet
My shadow wherever I go,
A more loving cat never was
The kindest, most gentle moggy I know.

Victoria Smith (12)
Wallace High School

A POLITICIAN

Like a teacher ready to answer,
Like a gun about to be fired,
Like a life hanging by a thread,
Like a mountaineer who can only keep climbing,
Like a beggar pleading public response,
Like a striker who must get the goal,
Like a storm that controls reality,
Like a ruler of his throne,
Like a God pulling against fate.

Stuart Ritchie (12)
Wallace High School

SHARKS

Sharks, hunters of the deep
Very, very rarely sleep.
Hunters not killers, that's what I say
Alone they patrol the ocean floor.

Scaring brave humans to the core
Really scary, for me not really
Sharks seem to be quiet scary
But for me no, not really.

Swimming through the ocean floor
Never is a bore
If I have one wish I would be a shark
So I could eat all the fish.

The hammerhead's head is a T
It's quite fascinating for me.
The hammerhead is quite weird
But it doesn't have a beard.

Sharks, hunters of the deep
Very, very rarely sleep
Sharks are fascinating to see
Especially for me.

Lee McCallum (12)
Wallace High School

THE RED FEAR RAPIDS OF LIFE

Fear is a long, stinging spike
That causes blood to flow out in steams
And runs down the jagged rocks
Which is life.

Alistair Boyd (13)
Wallace High School

FRIENDS

Friends are people who are kind,
Friends are people who understand you,
Friends are people who cheer you up when you are sad,
Friends are people who have a good laugh,
My friends are all of these,
My friends are the best.

Friends are like lambs in the spring,
Friends are like the golden sun,
Friends are like the springtime breeze.

Friends are like juicy strawberries,
Friends are like ice-cold juice,
Friends are like warm chocolate sauce.

Friends are like the good weather,
Friends are like the snow which is fun to play in,
Friends are like the water in a swimming pool.

Kirsty Dick (12)
Wallace High School

MY TEACHER

Like a ball that's always rolling,
Like me when I go bowling,
Like a bird that's always flying,
Like a chef who loves his frying,
Like a lion that's always roaring,
That's when I think school's boring,
Like a leopard that's always running,
Like a fox that's very cunning,
Like a bee that collects honey,
And for me that's very funny.

Tinashe Masocha (12)
Wallace High School

A Teacher

My teacher's like a ton of bricks, the way he shouts and roars.
My teacher's like a nippy wind, when she writes out detention slips.
My teacher's like a broken record, do this! Do that! Get out of there!
My teacher's like a wild, wild wolf, the way he prowls the corridor.
My teacher's like a baddie in the film, spoiling all the fun.
My teacher's like a red hot poker, you're scared to go too close.
My teacher's like an army sergeant, telling us what to do.
But best of all my teacher's like a sign post, showing us where to go.

Erica Mackie (12)
Wallace High School

Love

Love is a warm feeling you get inside yourself for another.
Love is special and tastes very nice.
It smells like a warm and rich perfume.
It looks like a warm and bright fire not too fierce.
It feels like a little butterfly flying around you.
It sounds like soft sounds of dolphins.
It's very smooth and delicate
And it's very nice to love someone,
Love is rich and warm . . .

Laura McKenna (12)
Wallace High School

Anger Is . . .

The feeling of rage and terror inside,
Your blood boiling like a volcanic eruption.
An explosion of sharp emotions,
The fiery feeling of sheer revenge.

Dominic Gillespie (12)
Wallace High School

240

HAPPINESS

Happiness is pink and orange,
It is an open flower,
It is like a peach,
It is soft like a cloud.

When I am happy, I like pink and orange,
When I am happy, I want to see an open flower,
When I am happy, I want to eat a peach,
When I am very happy, I want to go to the sky to touch a soft cloud.

Yasumi Takamiyagi (12)
Wallace High School

ANGER

Anger is the colour red,
It tastes of hatred and revenge,
It smells like disgust,
It feels as cold as steel and it's as sharp as a knife,
It cannot cut through flesh or bone,
But slices through emotion.

Russell King (13)
Wallace High School

JEALOUSY

A blackened-green abyss,
With jagged rusty metal for walls
And the smell of sawdust fills the air.
As I fall and fall into this abyss,
I start to feel something in my gut
This is jealousy.

Graeme Paris (14)
Wallace High School

LAUGHTER

Laughter is yellow,
Laughter is sweet,
Laughter is soft,
Laughter is the gurgling of water,
Laughter is tasty,
Laughter is bubbly,
Laughter is an Aero or Whispa,
Laughter is happy inside,
Laughter is sunny,
Laughter is clouds floating away,
Everyone should have laughter.

Mairi Laverty (12)
Wallace High School

SEA OF COLOURS

I gaze out and see,
A sea of colours,
Swaying in the wind
Looking cheerful and joyful.
I see yellows, oranges, reds,
There is a sweet smell
Wafting in the wind.
Whenever I feel down,
I gaze out and see
Waving cheerful waves
From the sea of colours below.

Lori Dempster (15)
Wallace High School

NIBBLES

Nibbles is my hamster
He's kind of brown and white,
He only comes out to play at night.
He runs round and round on this bright red wheel
And he drinks and eats lots for his meals.
Sometimes he is friendly
And sometimes he bites.
When he stands up on his feet,
I like to give him a treat.
I really like Nibbles my hamster.

Craig Allan (12)
Wallace High School

THE START

Tentatively, I stand and stare
Before me an ocean lies
Focus, don't blink.

Focus, don't blink
Ears primed
Muscles tense.

Muscles tense
I crouch to take my place
Silence.

Silence
Not a breath
The crack of a gun.

Ben Higson (15)
Wallace High School

A CHEATER

A cheater hates losing.

And when they win they are happy.

They feel good by winning.

When they win they have a rancid smell
Like what is left in the toilet after an Indian meal.

If they were food, they would taste like mud.

If they were a sound, it would be laughter pointed at you.

They look like the Devil, in my eyes anyway.

They feel hot and soggy if they get their way.

Daniel Jackson (12)
Wallace High School

MY MUM

Like a friend that you can talk to,
Like a shadow that you can follow,
Like a giant that you look up to,
Like a lion that is proud of you,
Like a jigsaw she's full of surprises!
Like a diamond that glistens in my eyes,
Like a waitress, she's very helpful!
Like a bird that loves to sing,
Like a hyena that can't stop laughing,
Like a brand new puppy that I adore!

Ashley Cummings (12)
Wallace High School

PRIDE FOR PREY

As I pad silently under the canopy
Watchful and alert, hunter and hunted
Looking for my prey.

Noise all around
Listening for a particular sound
Thunderous waterfalls camouflage my hunters.

As I covertly stalk my quarry
Closer and closer I shadow
Straight in for the kill.

I melt into the jungle
Majestically outwitting my hounders
For them to be such fools
As to capture me
To me they are meat.

For I am the hunter and they are the prey.

Nicola Hamilton (15)
Wallace High School

OFFICER BOB

Like an unstoppable roller coaster,
Like a racing car,
Like a blow of wind,
That blows clouds very far,
Like a spinning top just after it's been spun,
Like a fair that was made especially for fun,
Like rolling down a fifty foot hill,
Like a devil in the night,
He's a member of The Bill.

Douglas Murphy (12)
Wallace High School

THE LONELY MAN

The man sat down, there wasn't a sound
He was counting his money, pound by pound
He sat in the dark, without one single friend
And wished loneliness would come to an end.

His house was huge, was just like a mansion
And it had all the things, that were in fashion.
But one thing that was missing, was a very good friend
And wished his loneliness would come to an end.

But even with all his cars and money
The thing that the man, did not find funny
One thing he didn't have, was a very good friend
And he wished his loneliness would come to an end.

Iain McNicol (12)
Wallace High School

A STAR

Like a piece of golden light,
Like a spark of magic,
Like a sparkling ball,
Like a separate world,
Like a glow worm in the dark sky,
Like a million different places,
Like a shining piece of metal,
Like a piece of glitter,
Like a place waiting to be discovered.

Laura Johnston (11)
Wallace High School

THE LONELIEST MAN THAT COULD EVER BE

I'm the king of my castle
I have everything I want
But friends, I do not.
I sit on my throne
Drinking wine and eating cheese
But no one's there to share it with me
But little old me.
People all around me
But I feel so alone
I don't think anyone knows this
I wonder if they notice.
They think I'm fulfilled, content, happy and well, greedy,
But they don't know the real me.
I may be rich, but I'm the loneliest man that could ever be.

Lorna Robertson (13)
Wallace High School

A BOXER

This thing is a savage
And it's also very fast
It's sweaty and angry
In a fight, it won't come last.

It shouts and it grunts
After a win it will boast
And it will look like a beast
It may also celebrate from coast to coast.

Johnny Paterson (12)
Wallace High School

THE PENTAGON

A five-sided fortress,
The shield of America,
Liberty's guardian,
Vigilant and watchful,
The preserver of peace.

A five-sided foe,
The hammer of America,
Liberty's adversary,
Hostile and menacing,
Shape of oppression.

A five-sided moneymaker,
Food for the drones,
Sunshine holidays,
Comfort and security,
Monday till Friday, nine till five.

A five-sided target,
The heart of America,
The best prize for terrorists,
Only one way to crack it,
Bullseye!

Four sides not five,
A broken America,
Disbelief and loss,
Vulnerable but still we will become,
United and stronger.

Lara Thomas (15)
Wallace High School

BUTTERFLY

Sitting in the stadium
It's like a butterfly
Waiting for the game to start
Crowds of people having a lark.

The peaceful life of the butterfly was shattered when
Below it was a crowd of men.
The whistle blows to start the game
Everyone focused, they know their aim.

Sweet smells of the butterfly
People laugh, cheer and cry.
To score a goal is what needs done
You'd never guess this was meant to be fun.

Everyone yells
When a goal is scored.
The butterfly shakes
Like a volcano erupting.

All the bright colours of the football tops,
Crowds rippling up and down,
Like the fluttering wings of a butterfly
Fluttering low, fluttering high.

Again the whistle blows for the end of the game.
The butterfly begins to drain.
Now light enough to fly away
Crowds will be back another day.

Louise Rawding (15)
Wallace High School

FLUFFY COMPUTER

It smells like clothes, just been washed.
It's nice and fluffy.
It's big and beautiful.
It feels like a big, soft sponge.
It tastes like candyfloss.
It makes noises of killer whales.

Nicola Kaney (13)
Wallace High School

POEM

The almost perfect petals,
Surround the candle wick,
On the fiery coloured plant,
Melted raindrops lie,
As the candle
Burns to its death.

Katrina Button (15)
Wallace High School

UNTITLED

Anger feels like a huge bomb ticking
Away inside you just waiting to go
    Boooom
And anger tastes like very cold steel.

David Kerr (11)
Wallace High School

PANTHER

Crouching, waiting
Paws as big as plates
That pad slowly over twigs.
The yellow eyes deep
Like pools of gold.
The tail, long and curled
With a continuous twitch at the tip.
The body, long, sleek and black
Crouched low to the ground.
Muscles tense, pounce,
The bird doesn't stand a chance.

Dinner is served.

Megan Tully (12)
Wallace High School

THE SCHOOL LUNCHES

The lid is lifted off the pan,
The stew smells like fried mice,
The chips look a bit like a wrinkly old gran,
And the beans look decidedly like lice.
Sausages in a gravy mix,
Which looks like something off TV
It must be something they had to fix,
To keep us going till tea.
Mashed up greens look really mean,
Especially with the gruel,
The macaroni looks a pale green,
Why do they feed it us? To be cruel.

Then when it comes to the Blueberry Crunch,
I've just had enough . . . *I'm taking a packed lunch!*

Suzanne Higton (13)
Wellington School

MEMORIES

I remember crying every morning,
As if school were full of ghosts and ghouls
Instead of friends and friendly faces
Each morning I tried to get out of it
By escaping and hiding in the car or in the toilets.
The people couldn't have been nicer,
The surroundings better,
But still I yearned for the familiar home.

Home, the warm fire burning brightly,
The only place I ever wanted to be.
School was dark, full of unfamiliar sounds, unfamiliar faces.

I cried for weeks on end,
Afraid of what was round the next corner,
Then I found a best friend
Ten years later she is still my best friend
She was more lively, more outgoing, more vibrant than I.

She helped me progress,
She made me what I am today.

Claire Anderson (16)
Wellington School

CHOCOLATE

Sun peeking timidly over the horizon,
I was also getting up
Treading cautiously
Remembering to miss the third stair
Creeping, along the dark hallway.

The kitchen bathed in ghostly light
Chocolates, placed just out of reach
Fingers, trembling as I stretch up
Grasping the box with both hands.

The box, open in front of me
Greedily, I survey the treasure
Stolen, forbidden, unfamiliar
Carefully, I chose - only a few.

Caramel, orange, strawberry, toffee, praline,
Hazelnut, truffle, milk, dark, white
A mountain of shiny wrappers
An empty box,
A guilty face,
Hidden, behind chocolate covered hands.

Joanna Kerr (16)
Wellington School

THE NEVER-ENDING CYCLE OF LONELINESS

I stand there shaking in my new clothes,
New faces stare down at me and I smile weakly,
As I shut my eyes: I remember my last life with all my old friends,
I wish I could go back there, back to the old cycle but I can't.

The new classrooms with the new desks and chairs,
New teachers that look at me as if I were an orphan,
All around me giants push past me as if I were a bug on the floor,
I look back and wish I could go to the old days.

Now, those faces aren't so new,
The giants have left and I have become one,
No longer alone I have new friends that replace the old ones,
These few brief moments of happiness that will soon disappear.

Not long now till I have to start my journey again,
The cycle is complete and I have to move on,
The familiar faces and places will vanish while new ones appear,
Wishing you can go back, not wanting to go on.

Christopher Watt (15)
Wellington School

MOVING ON

We moved away from everything I had ever known,
To a place of strangeness, I didn't always understand.
The streets were lined with majestic trees, through which the sun shone,
freckling the pavements,
While young children played at their tremendous feet.

Nothing was far away; even school was a minute away on my
mother's hand.
Down the street, round the corner, to the menagerie of classrooms.
The playground was a forest, where I was a sapling in the
middle of a clearing.
Sometimes they noticed me and we could pretend anything.

Then I forgot my distress and learned fascinating new ideas.
My spelling book was crammed full of unpronounceable words;
I became happy and ran when the others did in childish glee;
It was so very simple then, with my carton of milk at break time.

Time marched on as the leaves fell twice during my time there.
We had to leave and I was glad because the adventure had ended.
There could be no more playing with conkers under the chestnut trees,
I was older
And leaving the trees for others, somewhere.

Abigail Martin (15)
Wellington School

254

TRAPPED

From my first word to my last goodnight
My young life is forever being watched.
As a child, my life is constantly changing,
Through the good times and the bad.
My wide smile seems forever scarred to my face
Feeling alone in this dark world,
Trying to overcome the greatest question of them all,
Death and what lies beyond?

Only time will bring the answer forth.
So life goes on awaiting that moment,
The moment I am free to let go of my fears,
And allow my greatest dreams to be released.
But how long does my suffering continue,
When will I awaken to the glaring sun,
Or will my eyes stay forever shut?
Only my heart will ever decide.

As night falls upon us and the sky is lit with anger,
I lie here alone collecting my thoughts,
Preparing for the moment of silence,
When the heavens open and the skies become clear,
Finally the time has come to forgive and forget,
A moment of prayer to the one I rely on,
Who has brought this torture to a finish
And allowed my life to come to an end.

Simon Murphy (15)
Wellington School

INNOCENCE LOST
(A reflection on childhood)

I remember dancing in the mid-day sun
Underneath the acorn trees beyond the hill
We were cartwheeling, laughing at the world
In an enchanted garden far from the school
I could smell the lawn, it was freshly mown
Blossom glided through the air.
I could smell the bark under the climbing frame
And the chlorine from the pool that stuck in our hair.
We squashed berries with the soles of our feet
To make patterns on the floor
And drew with chalk on the paving that lay outside the door
I see it now like a dream
Laughing and dancing in the sun
Beauty, which in extreme youth flowers but passes with the
summer's fun
We danced the maypole at the summer's fete
And around the bonfire on a summer's night.
It too danced and crackled and sang
As the fireworks flew momentarily bright
I remember it now as the seasons change and the world is touched
with white

The sounds so clear and the vision so pure
I remember that garden bathed in sunlight.

Kristine Kozicki (15)
Wellington School

WHEN I WAS YOUNGER

Our room was great.
It had the doll's house and the piano
And it was big and when
We finished our work we would
Dress up and play in the house.
It was fun then but it didn't last forever.
Does anything?

The house was big to us then,
And it even had an upstairs.
We could be adults,
But were forbidden to go upstairs,
Which we could never understand.
We were proper kids and are we still now?

Soon the bell would ring, loud in our heads,
So we went outside and played some more.
We ran around: kids
Enjoying our childish ways.
Those times were good,
No need to care or worry about anything.

Our teacher scared us.
She was nice but put us in the corner
If we were bad. I was once.
I kept talking, like I always do.
That wasn't very fair - but now
I realise it was my fault, I was being childish.

Time passed and we grew older,
Leaving our childish ways behind us.
People moved away, people moved on.
All of a sudden - we had grown up.
It's clear now that nothing lasts forever.

Mary Howie (16)
Wellington School

GLOBE TROTTING

I went holidaying
In the South of France.
The food was yucky
But the sand was grand
And on the beach
There was a band.

I went on holiday
To South Africa.
I went to Table Mountain
And climbed to the top.
I saw all of Cape Town
Then I went down.

I went on holiday
To sunny Portugal.
In a restaurant
I saw Thomas Flogel
Who plays for Hearts
And I played him at darts.

On the journey home
I felt depressed.
But then I thought
I like home
I like my little garden
Where there stands my gnome.

Steven Coyle (12)
Woodfarm High School

DISASTER

The music of footsteps, the drone of voices
The clatter of suitcases, the screams from children,
The doors slam violently, the plane starts to quiver,
Ready to take-off, to fly over the river,
The plane starts to fly, the clouds begin to form
Where we are going, no one is informed
But something is happening, there's something not right
The faces of passengers twist in fright
My legs push me up, my hands clutch the seat,
My eyes wander further as the passengers retreat,
I realise what's happening, I ask myself why,
It's been taken over by hijackers, I just wanna die.

We've been flying for a while now, ladies collapse in stress
I try to get up and help but my foot catches on a lady's dress,
A phone's being passed round, I get it at last,
I'm dialling my wife's number, I'd better do it fast,
She answers the phone, I tell her what's wrong,
She never ceases crying or telling me to be strong,
I tell her I love her, I always will,
The signal cuts us off, I'm all alone,
But that is nothing to what's happening now,
I glance out the window, we're above New York,
We're plummeting down, towards a large building,
We're never going to make it, we're all gonna die,
The children begin to cry and cry,
We've not got long now, we're ten metres away,
My life's gonna end here, I'll just pray and pray.

Barbara Jamieson (12)
Woodfarm High School

FANTASTIC JOURNEYS

All the fantastic journeys,
My eyes alone have seen,
All the amazing countries,
And the beautiful hills of green.

All the fantastic journeys
The blue waves of splashing water,
All the amazing countries,
The sun keeps getting hotter.

All the fantastic journeys,
The sights of old and new,
All the amazing countries,
Seems like they're there for me and you.

All the fantastic journeys,
The wind, the rain, the sun,
All the amazing countries,
I'm still having so much fun.

Karen McKenzie (11)
Woodfarm High School

ACROSS THE LAGOON

In a crowd, sore feet, sore head,
Tired already, the day just beginning,
The boat arrives, a scramble for seats.

Excited tourists, maps and guidebooks,
What will it be like?
Beautiful buildings, canals and boats.

At last it comes into sight,
Everything I expected and more,
The bells of San Marco ring out a welcome.

Pigeons fly around my head,
Wings beating, beady eyes glinting greedily
Happy and at home . . . in Venice.

Stuart Miller (12)
Woodfarm High School

THE CIRCLE OF LIFE

Bright lights, loud noises,
Suddenly I'm here,
New life, new world,
Nothing to fear.

Bright lights, loud noises,
School days are here,
Can't stand the teacher,
Everything to fear.

Bright lights, loud noises,
I've got a career.
Can't stand the pace
Stress is here.

Bright lights, loud noises,
The end is near
Come get me God
Nothing to fear.

Kirsten Nixon (11)
Woodfarm High School

Florida's the Place to Be

Disney World's a wonder world
Mickey Mouse and Minnie Mouse
With lots of rides and wonderful sights
And lots of delicious tasty bites.

Universal Studios is a great day out
Lots to do out and about.
Lots of exciting thrills and spills
And heroes sitting on top of the hill.

Movie rides are the greatest
And some are of the wettest
With cartoons that are spectacular
MGM's the place to be.

Gillian Treacy (12)
Woodfarm High School

Rush

The businessmen at Heathrow,
Always know where to go.
Every morning on the train,
Every day, always the same!

Children on the way to school
Lifeguards going to the swimming pool,
Ladies of charities doing good works,
Marks and Spencer's selling shirts.

Eight o'clock on the dot
The traffic always comes to a stop.
Why is everyone in such a hurry?
Really there's no need to worry.

January, February, March or May,
Whatever week, whatever day
Whether it be rain or shine,
They always have to be on time!

Kathryn Brackenridge (13)
Woodfarm High School

CHIMPS

Chimpanzees are funky
They swing from trees all day
Bananas are their favourite food
They play and play and play.

Although I hate bananas,
I'd really love a chimp
I'd give it sausages and chips
'Cause bananas are for wimps!

The zoo would come and capture it
Then I would be very upset
My chimp would be locked up in a cage
And I would have no pet!

Andy Rogerson (12)
Woodfarm High School

LYING IN MY BED AT NIGHT

Lying in my bed at night,
At only five-past ten,
I hear voices out of my window,
Oh! How I wish I was them.

Lying in my bed at night,
I wish that I was up,
To run about and scream and shout,
Or just to get a cup

Of tea or a glass of water,
Though I'm supposed to be asleep,
I have a really dry throat,
So I think that I might creep

Downstairs,
But I hear footsteps in the hall,
I can't do it anymore,
I climb back into bed like a sleepyhead,
Listening to the footsteps getting closer to the door.

Then all goes quiet, everything is still,
And I am left lying there waiting,
Waiting for tomorrow to come,
So that I can have some fun!

Louise Robin (11)
Woodfarm High School

BACK IN TIME

I stepped on the podium,
As I was told to,
And waited
I don't know what for
But I waited.

Maybe I wasn't waiting,
But I was hesitating.
Too scared to take the other big step
Scared of what was going to happen
But I waited.

I think I was waiting to be told,
Told what to do
Whether to go on or stop
I wanted to run away
But I waited.

I still don't know what I was doing
Waiting, hesitating or wanting to be shown the way
But to this day I am still waiting
Waiting to be shown the way.

Sehrish Bashir (12)
Woodfarm High School